Developing a hapi Edge

A Rich Node.js Framework for Apps and Services

Van Nguyen, Daniel Bretoi, Wyatt Preul, Lloyd Benson

Developing a hapi Edge

ISBN 9781939902207
Published by: Bleeding Edge Press, Santa Rosa, CA 95404
Title: Developing a hapi Edge
Authors: Van Nguyen, Daniel Bretoi, Wyatt Preul, Lloyd Benson
Editor: Troy Mott
Copy Editor: Christina Rudloff
Typesetter: Bob Herbstman
Website: bleedingedgepress.com

Table of Contents

Foreword

A framework that makes you hapi

From the very beginning, hapi was built around a simple philosophy--
development should be fun. The role of a framework is to increase your
productivity and step in when you want it, but step aside when you
don't. It should not mess around with your environment, nor should it
take away any of the power available from the underlying platform. But
more importantly, the role of a framework is to establish a foundation
for collaboration.

Enterprise software development has earned the notoriety of a painful, bureaucratic, stale, and complicated process. What's worse is that
we have learned to accept it as the status quo. At the center of the problem is the fact that enterprise software development happens in large
teams, often distributed organizationally and geographically, and require a significant amount of process to prevent one mistake from affecting the productivity of hundreds of developers, or worse affecting the
business operations.

When I set course building hapi, I knew the framework had to be the
best at handling the typical web application activities, such as authentication, state, and caching, but those are all prerequisites for just being a
contender. The real core of the framework is its functionality aimed at
making large scale development easier, and fun. It means paying attention to small details like protecting the developer from creating conflicts
in routes, cookies or other named properties, and to big details like how
to allow teams to work on the same application without constant coordi-
nation.

As the project matured, hapi itself became a large scale development
process. With dozens of contributes from many different companies and
a growing code base, we had to expand the reach of our hapi-ness cen-
tric philosophy to the full development process. We greatly value code
quality and consistency, and since writing tests was usually a painful

part of software development, we worked to make that better, stream-lined, and enjoyable. We wrote new testing tools, fortified our coding style, and automated much of the tedious parts. We did the same for documentation, automating the process as much as possible to free developers to focus on functionality.

Four years into the project, the satisfaction of its community is still the greatest motivator and guide in moving the work forward. As it continue to mature, we learn more every day about how it is being used and how we can continue to evolve it; hapi is a dynamic community and the project has a history of not being afraid to break things in order to make them better. We refuse to accept the status quo, even our own.

I am excited you are taking the time to learn about hapi and consider it for your next project; hapi is a community project and you are now part of it. Your voice and your hapi-ness matter and you should consider this your very personal invitation to join us, ask questions, and share with us how we can make things better.

Eran Hammer

July 2015

Preface

Why use hapi?

"A rich framework for building applications and services hapi enables developers to focus on writing reusable application logic instead of spending time building infrastructure."

   -- **hapijs.com**

   hapi is a web development framework designed for the rapid development of RESTful services APIs using JavaScript. While it is also simple and easy to use, hapi also includes a lot of features out-of-the-box that typically come from third-party tools, features like input validation, caching, authentication, etc.

   Developers use hapi because it is easy to use, stable, robust, well-tested (and battle-tested by WalmartLabs during Black Friday), and powerful. It is specifically designed to work well in enterprise environments where multiple teams will work on individual or overlapping pieces that connect together. hapi does this by enabling developers to focus on writing reusable, modular code without forcing them to do so in a very narrowly defined way.

What should you know prior to reading this book?

Readers should be comfortable with JavaScript, Node.js, and the design and implementation of basic websites and web applications.

Source code/sample app

Throughout the book, we will be referencing code from our sample application: hapi-plugins.com. hapi-plugins.com is a searchable repository of hapi-related modules available on NPM. You can view the complete source code at **https://github.com/hapijs-edge/hapi-plugins.com**. You can see the completed application at **https://hapi-plugins.com**).

What will this book teach you?

This book will teach you how to build awesome web applications using hapi. It covers many aspects of how and why hapi works the way it does. You will see helpful and advanced features such as authentication, validation, caching, templating, testing, and debugging. In this book, you will also walk through the creation of a fully operational hapi web application.

Authors

Daniel Bretoi

Daniel Bretoi is a contractor @WalmartLabs where he worked on Eran Hammer's team, which developed the hapi framework. He has worked in the industry for 15 years and favors interpreted languages. In 2002 he was an early adopter of Ruby and generally embraces new technologies.

Wyatt Preul

Wyatt Preul is a software developer for Walmart. He is one of the core maintainers of the hapi node.js framework. At Walmart, Wyatt was one of the investigators of the now infamous node.js memory leak. In addition to this, he has helped deliver many node.js projects within Walmart. Apart from his day job Wyatt loves all things node, web app security, archery, coffee roasting, and beer brewing.

Van Nguyen

Van Nguyen is a Senior Software Engineer, Full-Stack, IDEA (Big Data) at Intuit. He is currently hacking on JavaScript UIs for managing and visualizing Big Data.

Lloyd Benson

Lloyd Benson is a consultant at Walmart. He is also the owner of Open Source Infrastructure LLC.

Technical reviewers

We would like to the thank the following technical reviewers for their early feedback and careful critiques: Doron Pagot, Troy Whiteley, Jeffrey Jagoda, Colin Ihrig, Daniel Barnes, Michael Caputo, James Butler, Alvin Teh, Josh Mock, Michael Parks, Jonathan Holmlund, Glenn Jones, and Jesse Newcomer.

Introduction to hapi 1

History

hapi's origin would start at Yahoo! late in the year of 2010 on a project called Sled. Sled was a collaborative list-making tool written as an experiment to explore empowerment through restrictions by Eran Hammer. Sled was written in node and Eran fell in love with the technology. Sled was eventually shut down and was generously open-sourced by Yahoo! as Postmile in August of 2011. Wanting to continue with node, Eran left for Walmart where he took the good parts of Postmile and hapi was born on the 5th of August, 2011. Tasked with working on a web services layer, the development of hapi continued at Walmart. The original versions in hapi used the Express framework. However, it was eventually realized that there were limitations with Express that made it not suitable for the particular requirements faced at Walmart. While Express was great, it was missing a lot of things and hapi evolved to it's own stand-alone framework.

The name hapi comes from HTTP API server, and once the name was repeated, the connection to Ren & Stimpy was made, a cult cartoon from cartoon network. The **"Happy Happy Joy Joy Song"** was featured in many of the early presentations of hapi.

With the Ren and Stimpy theme in mind, other tools in the hapi.js framework started referencing the show in one way or another, with the ultimate goal is that coding should be fun we as coders can be a bit silly when we write code even though we're put in large enterprise environments. Relax, and have a bit of fun.

Feature-wise, hapi was designed to prevent recurring problems experienced with other frameworks at the time. That included problems like: middleware ordering problems, lack of isolation, slow path matching, testability, and lack of commonly used built-in features. Middleware ordering problems are solved by the hapi Request Lifecycle, which provides controlled, dependency-mapped hook points throughout the life of a request from when it hits the server, to after a response is returned to the user. The lack of isolation was solved by domains and later replaced with an even better system. Path matching in hapi is built for speed and flexibility. hapi code is testable from start to finish (and is well-tested, itself!). Finally, via the hapi.js universe (**https://github.com/hapijs**), there are dozens of official hapi plugins that are as robust, well-tested, and flexible as hapi itself. This is in addition to the hundreds of community modules available on NPM.

Designed and built entirely in open-source, hapi has also set a very high bar for open source projects. From the thoroughly complete code coverage (a process ingrained from the beginning thanks to Wyatt Preul) to incredibly detailed release notes and well-organized documentation, anyone using hapi and related modules can trust that it works reliably and behaves as expected.

hapi has an incredibly **long list of satisfied users** - not least of which is WalmartLabs itself, who has prided itself on having the largest Node.js deployment in the world thanks to **Black Friday**.

There are a lot of reasons to use hapi. Try it and you will see what a pleasant experience developing web applications in Node.js can be.

> hapi was able to handle all of Walmart mobile Black Friday traffic with about 10 CPU cores and 28Gb RAM (of course we used more but they were sitting idle at 0.75% load most of the time). This is mind blowing traffic going through VERY little resources. -- Eran Hammer, **https://github.com/hapijs/hapi/issues/1326**

Book overview

This book will take you through the process of developing a basic web application with hapi. We will be building a searchable repository of hapi plugins. A live demo is available at **hapi-plugins.com**.

The first seven chapters are all about creating and configuring a hapi server. These chapters also cover a lot more tangential information in case you need to build in or use a feature not found in hapi-plugins.com. The next two chapters (8, 9) cover how to obtain data, process it, and format it. The last three chapters (10, 11, 12) cover some more advanced topics including some very useful industry best practices.

1. Introduction

   This first chapter introduces hapi, the book overview, coding style guidelines, and a short walkthrough of the demo application.

2. Server

   This chapter focuses on the configuration of a hapi server. It also covers commonly used best practices, examples, and how to customize within the request lifecycle.

3. Routes

   Routes map URIs to code. In this chapter, you will gain a thorough understanding of how to match complicated patterns.

4. Handlers

   Handlers are functions responsible for receiving a request from users and returning a response. In this chapter, you will see all of the different ways hapi can respond to requests.

5. Validation

   Validation (through Joi) is another amazingly helpful feature of hapi. This chapter illustrates just how powerful validation is and how it can make developers' lives easier.

6. Plugins

   Plugins are middleware done "right." This chapter shows you how plugins enable cross-functional, remote teams to work together without causing any of the problems typically associated with middleware.

7. Authentication

   This chapter provides a thorough step-by-step walkthrough of how to enable authentication and set cookies.

8. Models

This chapter walks through connecting to a third-party RESTful API for use in your hapi web application. Then, it also walks through connecting to a MongoDB database for use in your hapi web application. It also showcases examples of how to operate in two other popular databases (Cassandra & PostgreSQL).

9. Templating

In this chapter, you will see how to separate data from presentation in the handlers' responses.

10. Testing

Testing is often misunderstood or difficult to learn. This chapter will empower you to add tests to your web application, which improves robustness and code quality.

11. Debugging

This chapter walks through some of the hard-earned debugging tricks we've learned running one of the largest Node.js deployments in the world. In this chapter, you will learn how to inspect a running service, track statistics, trace memory leaks, and identify other problems.

12. Security

This chapter covers some industry best practices regarding securing your web application.

13. Appendix

This chapter stores the appendix with descriptions and code examples for other selected databases, and templating engines.

hapi-plugins.com

In this book, we will walk through how to use hapi to create the back-end services for a real (but basic) web application, hapi-plugins. hapi-plugins (**hapi-plugins.com**) is a searchable repository for hapi-related modules available on NPM.

This book will **NOT** cover how to build the client-side JavaScript portion of the application. However, the complete **source code** is available on **GitHub**.

Style

We will be following hapi style-guidelines throughout this book. To find more about what they are, you can see them at the **hapi Style Guide**.

We may not agree with everything in the styles, but it's worth noting that just having this style guide to follow prevents time taken up by discussion. It's 99 percent good. Some practices may look odd, but it really helps with the visualization of the code. We recommend choosing this style not only for projects related to hapi, but for node development in general.

We are relentlessly strict about our guidelines when it comes to style. Style is something that should be one of the simplest concepts in programming to actually follow, yet we've found many get sloppy. If you can't follow the simple things, then it shows you're not paying attention to what you're doing. Therefore, we've taken to the idea that the further away the code is from the style, the closer the code needs to be scruti-nized during code review.

In addition to ending up with clear and concise code throughout the programs (which is a blessing on its own), we also pay close attention during code reviews trying to find anything that's out of place. That forces us to scan every single line. This is a good thing because it helps catch oddities not just on a large scale, but smaller bugs as well.

Summary

Without further ado, let us begin in the next chapter with the hapi server.

Server 2

hapi is a framework used for building applications and services. Behind every service, there is a server; something that serves what the client needs. hapi is at its core a superset of an HTTP server. Everything around hapi is tied in to this fact, so we kick off this book talking about the main functionality. It's from this that everything else is configured and makes a difference. We're going to be talking about a lot of concepts that are related to the server, plugins, handlers, testing, and more.

In this chapter we look at how to set up a server and how we've set up the server for our hapi-plugins.com example. We're going to teach you the ins and outs of the server in the hapi framework. You'll learn the different ways of running a hapi server in production. You'll know how to set up caching. You'll get a first glimpse into plugins and how to add methods that will be available throughout your application. Finally you will learn about the request lifecycle and how to add custom functions for your application.

Setting up a simple server

Of course while we can start a book off without having a hello world example, we're not going to. It's important to know how to set up a server in its simplest configuration before advancing to more complex setups.

```
var Hapi = require('hapi');

var server = new Hapi.Server();

server.connection();

server.route({
    method: 'GET',
    path: '/',
```

```
    handler: function (request, reply) {

        return reply('hello hapi');
    }
});

server.start(function (err)  {

    console.log(server.info.uri);
});
```

Here we created an instance of a hapi server. We don't actually have to do anything at all to configure it. The next step is to get a connection to the server. The connection is the port and host that the server is listening to. By default, the host is set to localhost and the port is generated randomly based on ports that don't require system administrator access to use, and that are available. Since we don't know what the port is, we print the URI out at the end so that we can see where our server is listening.

We add a route so that we have somewhere we can actually send a request to. We'll go a lot further into routes in Chapter 3, but for now, think of a route as a configured path that the request from the client (browser) can take in order to have a particular response served.

At this point we start the server, and log the server URI so that we know what port the server started on.

The next logical steps would be to set a port for our server to start on so that we know it's the same each time. This can be accomplished by using the options for the connection: server.connection({ port: 8088 });

Setting up the server for hapi-plugins.com

Now that we have a more basic understanding of how to set up a server, let's examine what we'll need to do to set up the server for hapi-plugins.com.

A typical architecture for a Single Page Application (SPA) is to have some HTML templates served up through a front-end framework such as Ember, AngularJS, React or otherwise. We've chosen to use React for our front-end. The information served to the framework can use the same back-end methods of serving up the data to the framework, but a cleaner approach is to have a separate API server handle the data and this is the approach that we have decided to take.

```
var internals = {
    servers: {
        http: {
            port: 8080,
            host: '0.0.0.0',
            labels: ['http']
        },
        api: {
            port: 8088,
            host: '0.0.0.0',
            labels: ['api']
        }
    },
    options: {
        files: {
            relativeTo: __dirname
        }
    }
};
```

We're putting the main HTTP server on port 8080 and the API server on port

1. They're both running and listening on 0.0.0.0 which is used for binding to all ip addresses for the connections. When the server starts up, this will only be running one node process. The labels in the configuration are for labeling the connection so that the appropriate plugins can be loaded. hapi is a framework that's plugin-centric, meaning that everything is designed to be composed using plugins. You can find out more details about plugins in Chapter 6, but for now, let's realize it's an important concept. All of the methods available on the server are also available on anything passed to the plugin. It's the first argument passed to a plugin register object. Sometimes the argument name is plugin and other times it's server. We will call it a plugin.

For hapi-plugins.com we are setting up two connections for our server. One is for HTML content, and the other is for our API content.

```
var Async = require('async');
var Bell = require('bell');
var Blipp = require('blipp');
var Hapi = require('hapi');
var HapiAuthCookie = require('hapi-auth-cookie');
var Hoek = require('hoek');
var Api = require('./api');
var Authentication = require('./authentication');
var Controllers = require('./controllers');
```

```
var Models = require('./models');
var Routes = require('./routes');

var internals = {
    servers: {
        http: {
            port: 8080,
            host: '0.0.0.0',
            labels: ['http']
        },
        api: {
            port: 8088,
            host: '0.0.0.0',
            labels: ['api']
        }
    },
    options: {
        files: {
            relativeTo: __dirname
        }
    }
};


exports.init = function (callback) {

    var server = new Hapi.Server();
    server.connection(internals.servers.http);
    server.connection(internals.servers.api);
    //...

};
```

We begin by loading our libraries that we're going to use. We've organized our code as Models, Routes, and Controllers. We also have code specifically for our API.

What's new here are the labels. They serve as an indicator for the system that can be used to decide what plugins will be loaded for each connection later on. We are likely to only have some plugins listen to one connection and not the other. Some may want to listen to both, such as a /heartbeat type call, but in general unless one is only using SSL/TSL and the other unencrypted, there should be little duplication. You can read more about how to select plugins and how to manage plugins in Chapter 6. This is done using the server.register().

```
server.path(internals.options.files.relativeTo);

server.on('request-error', function (request, response) {

    console.log('request-error:');
    console.dir(response);
});
```

server.path indicates to hapi a path prefix so that we can use relative paths to locate files and templates.

We also set up an event for handling errors that happen on requests.

```
var registerHttpPlugins = function (next) {

    server.register([
        Bell,
        Blipp,
        HapiAuthCookie,
        Authentication,
        Controllers,
        Models,
        Routes
    ],
    { select: 'http' },
    function (err) {

        return next(err);
    });
};

var registerApiPlugins = function (next) {

    server.register([
        Blipp,
        Controllers,
        Models,
        Api
    ],
    { select: 'api' },
    function (err) {

        return next(err);
    });
};

Async.auto({
    http: registerHttpPlugins,
    api: registerApiPlugins
```

```
    }, function (err, data) {

        if (err) {
            console.log('server.register err:', err);
            return callback(err);
        }

        server.start(function () {

            return callback(null, server);
        });
    });

    exports.init(Hoek.ignore);
```

This is a big chunk of code to take in all at once, but it's all related, so bear with us while we explain what we're trying to achieve. First, the goal is to register our plugins and start our server. We have designed our code to use plugins in order to separate it into manageable chucks. Some of this is unfamiliar, but it will become clear here and in the chapters to come.

Now that we know what we're trying to accomplish, let's see how it's done. `registerHttpPlugins` and `registerApiPlugins` are functions to handle registering the plugins for the two separate connections on our server. One function can only apply plugins to one connection at a time. Therefore, we need to distinguish these two functions because we have configured hapi to have two connections.

We're using Async.auto to accomplish this asynchronously, which we can get away with because it doesn't matter in what order we register plugins. If you're not familiar with the **Async** library, it's a great tool, and we use it everywhere for cleaner code. It's worth stopping here and taking a break to look at the documentation for **Async** to get familiarized with it. We'll wait.

If there are errors, we print the error to the console and exit. If there are no errors, we go ahead and start the server.

Note that server.register can take an array of plugins. This behavior is similar to [Async].series. In fact, hapi is internally using a lightweight version of Async called **items**. If you're not finding yourself using all of the features of Async, then this may be a good alternative for you.

As you can see, setting up the server can be quite an ordeal. There's a lot to keep track of. There is however, a much cleaner approach. Next up, we're going to have a look at the glue, rejoice, and confidence modules.

Glue

Glue is a way to compose server settings. Often it's desired to have server configuration stay out of code because it's far more predictable.

What we have above is a rather complicated set up. In order to make what we have easier we're going to use `glue`. Below is how we do that.

```
// Load modules

var Glue = require('glue');
var Hapi = require('hapi');


// Internals

var internals = {
    manifest: {
        connections: [{
            port: 8080,
            labels: ['http']
        },
        {
            port: 8088,
            labels: ['api']
        }],
        plugins: {
            bell: [{ 'select': 'http' }],
            blipp: [{}],
            'hapi-auth-cookie': [{ 'select': 'http' }],
            './authentication': [{ 'select': 'http' }],
            './controllers': [{ 'select': ['http', 'api' ]}],
            './models': [{ 'select': ['http', 'api']}],
            './routes': [{ 'select': ['http']}],
            './api': [{ 'select': ['api']}],
            good: {
                opsInterval: 5000,
                reporters: [{
                    'reporter': 'good-console',
                    'events': { 'ops': '*', 'log': '*' }
                }]
            }
        }
    }
};


Glue.compose(internals.manifest,
```

```
    { relativeTo: __dirname }, function (err, server) {

    if (err) {
        console.log('server.register err:', err);
    }
    server.start(function(){
        console.log('server started');
    });
});
});
```

This is the entire server file with all of the requires included. It is much cleaner to understand and follow, as you can see. Previously, before glue, we had to define two functions to apply plugins to each connection (http and api). With glue, we define all of the plugins in one place and give each plugin an array containing the connection(s). Glue will automatically apply the plugins to the right connection(s) as defined.

Rejoice

Rejoice is a CLI tool to start up a hapi instance from a purely JSON configuration. This module was split off and used to be in hapi itself as bin/ hapi. It is pretty straight forward. Now that we have learned about how glue composition works, you simply need the JSON result of the manifest that was mentioned. This results in:

```
{
    "connections": [{
        "port": 8080,
        "labels": ["http"]
    },
    {
        "port": 8088,
        "labels": ["api"]
    }],
    "plugins": {
        "bell": [{ "select": "http" }],
        "blipp": [{}],
        "hapi-auth-cookie": [{ "select": "http" }],
        "./authentication": [{ "select": "http" }],
        "./controllers": [{ "select": ["http", "api" ]}],
        "./models": [{ "select": ["http", "api"]}],
        "./routes": [{ "select": ["http"]}],
        "./api": [{ "select": ["api"]}],
        "good": {
            "opsInterval": 5000,
```

```
      "reporters": [{
          "reporter": "good-console",
          "events": { "ops": "*", "log": "*" }
      }]
    }
  }
}
```

Since this is a json file we have used double quotes. Assuming you have installed rejoice locally, you can start it up with `rejoice -c example.json`. It's nice to be able to work with a single JSON file, but you may find that you want to do things differently depending on environment. This is where `confidence` comes in.

Confidence

Confidence is another CLI tool. You can take a JSON file and apply filters to it so you can process that file. Managing multiple files per environment can not only be tedious but prone to errors. You may add a new setting to one of these files but forget to add it to the others. This leads to configuration drift problems and with `confidence` you can be 'confident' that you have just one location to go to as the source of truth. Let's take a look at our rejoice file and apply filters to it that we can generate with `confidence`.

```
{
    "connections": [{
        "port": 8080,
        "labels": ["http"]
    },
    {
        "port": 8088,
        "labels": ["api"]
    }],
    "plugins": {
        "$filter": env,
        "$base": {
            "bell": [{ "select": "http" }],
            "hapi-auth-cookie": [{ "select": "http" }],
            "./authentication": [{ "select": "http" }],
            "./controllers": [{ "select": ["http", "api" ]}],
            "./models": [{ "select": ["http", "api"]}],
            "./routes": [{ "select": ["http"]}],
            "./api": [{ "select": ["api"]}],
```

```
            "good": {
                "opsInterval": 5000
            }
        },
        "dev": {
            "blipp": [{}],
            "good": {
                "reporters": [{
                    "reporter": "good-console",
                    "events": { "ops": "*", "log": "*" }
                }]
            }
        },
        "prod": {
            "good": {
                "reporters": [{
                    "reporter": "good-file",
                    "events": { "log": "*" },
                    "config": "/path/to/log.log"
                },
                {
                    "reporter": "good-file",
                    "events": { "ops": "*" },
                    "config": "/path/to/ops.log"
                }]
            }
        }
    }
}
```

Here you can have filters setup for the dev and prod keywords. To generate a JSON file we can later use for rejoice you can run: confidence -c confidence.json --filter.env=dev > rejoice.json. This will result in merging what's in $base with the dev specific entries. In this case, you want blipp and good-console for only the development environment because they are handy for debugging. You don't want these in your prod environment however. For prod you've added good-file that logs your output to a file, which can later be processed to a log aggregator (see discussion in Chapter 11). To generate the prod config file, you do the same confidence command as before but change the filter to be --filter.env=prod. Many times it's convenient during a deploy to generate this on the fly and just ensure you have the some valid output before you start up your server. Invalid JSON will result in errors. Also you will see that the opsInterval setting in $base will get merged for both filters.

Confidence can do even more, but this should empower you to have one configuration for your hapi server so you can easily maintain your environments. Using **confidence** in combination with **rejoice** (which uses **glue**) will keep your ever-changing environment needs manageable.

Server methods

You may want to register methods that are available everywhere on the server for access. Doing this is very easy as shown here.

```
server.method('spumko', function (next) {

    console.log('the hapijs project was');
    console.log('originally called spumko');
    return next(null, 'called');
});
```

The server methods are then accessed via the **server.methods** object.

```
server.methods.spumko(function (err, result) {

    console.log(result); // prints "called"
});
```

You may not want your method to require a callback. If so, you can toggle this behavior in one of the options.

```
server.method('spumko', function (arg) {

    console.log('the hapijs project was');
    console.log('originally called spumko');

    return 'called';
}, { callback: false });

console.log(server.methods.spumko()); // prints "called"
```

The additional options that are available are bind, cache and generateKey.

bind sets the context for the method and defaults to the context when the method was created. If you want some other context, this is the place to do it.

cache has the same configuration, which will be discussed in Configuring for caching.

Finally, generateKey is a function that's used to create a unique key for caching purposes.

Decorating the server

Using server.decorate, you can add functions directly to the server object. This is different from server.method where you add methods to be accessed via server.methods. In addition to decorating the server object, you can also decorate the reply object, and we'll cover that specifically in Chapter 4.

```
server.decorate('server', 'success', function () {

    return this.response({ success: true });
});
```

Configuring for caching

We can use server.cache to setup a cache. hapi has a built-in server cache facility and it relies on the hapi plugin **catbox**. By default, there is a built-in memory cache **catbox-memory** but other types of cache engines are supported like redis, mongoDB, memcached, and others. Please refer to the catbox documentation for more details on these strategies. Here is a simple example of how to use server.cache.

```
var cache = server.cache({
    segment: 'plugins',
    expiresIn: 60 * 60 * 1000
});

cache.set('pluginName', { author: 'mindy' }, null, function (err) {

    cache.get('pluginName', function (err, value, cached, log) {

        // value === { author: 'mindy' };
```

```
    });
});
```

Here we have setup a cache, with a segment of `plugins`. Segments are used to isolate cached items within the cache partition. When you call this within a plugin, it defaults to `!name` where `name` is the name of the plugin.

We also have an expiresIn setting, which is set to expire the cached item in one hour. There is also an interesting setting called `staleIn` where you can mark the item stored in cache as stale. This setting must be less than expiresIn. Using this feature, you can have the cache ready to go by the time expiresIn comes along. If `staleIn` doesn't have sufficient time before expiresIn is hit, it will just work like the usual expiresIn. This is like warming up your cache.

Finally, you can see that we use `cache.set()` to set the key `plugin-Name` with the value of the `author` object and we can retrieve that value using the `cache.get()` method.

There are more options to server.cache and to get more details visit the hapijs.com **documentation**.

Request lifecycle

Understanding how a technology handles an HTTP request is fundamental in developing secure, efficient applications using that technology. Node.js itself doesn't provide much in this regard, although creating a server is fairly simple in Node.js:

```
var server = require('http');

server.on('request', function (request, response) {

    // do something
});

server.listen(80);
```

That's it, just a function. The request has all of the inbound information from the origin of the request, and the reply has a writeable stream that needs to have headers set, information written to it, and then have the connection closed. At first this can be exciting, especially for those who haven't dealt with it in the past. Once an application needs a routing table however, it becomes a lot more taxing to deal with.

The way in which hapi deals with the requests is by having a reliable series of events happen each time a request is received by the server. Here's the full lifecycle:

- **'onRequest'** extension point
  - ☒ always called
  - ☒ the request object passed to the extension functions is decorated with the `request.setUrl()` and `request.setMethod()` methods. Calls to these methods will impact how the request is routed and can be used for rewrite rules.
  - ☒ `request.route` is not yet populated at this point.
  - ☒ JSONP configuration is ignored for any response returned from the extension point since no route is matched yet and the JSONP configuration is unavailable.
- Lookup route using request path
- Parse cookies
- **'onPreAuth'** extension point
- Authenticate request
- Read and parse payload
- Authenticate request payload
- **'onPostAuth'** extension point
- Validate path parameters
- Process query extensions (e.g. JSONP)
- Validate query
- Validate payload
- **'onPreHandler'** extension point
- Route prerequisites - configured in the Handler
- Route handler
- **'onPostHandler'** extension point
  - ☒ The response object contained in `request.response` may be modified (but not assigned a new value). To return a different response type (for example, replace an error with an HTML response), return a new response via `reply(response)`.
- Validate response payload
- **'onPreResponse'** extension point
  - ☒ always called (except when `reply.close()` is called or the client terminates the connection prematurely).

- ☒ The response contained in `request.response` may be modified (but not assigned a new value). To return a different response type (for example, replace an error with an HTML response), return a new response via `reply(response)`. Note that any errors generated after `reply(response)` is called will not be passed back to the `'onPreResponse'` extension method to prevent an infinite loop.

- Send response (may emit `'request-error'` event)
- Emits `'response'` event
- Wait for tails
- Emits `'tail'` event

Extension points

Now that we've discussed the lifecycle, we can utilize 'extension points' in hapi. These 'extension points' expose streams in the lifecycle where other functions can be inserted. They can easily be tied to a server to augment the existing hapi lifecycle. We use the `server.ext` functionality to accomplish this. Let's look at a couple of examples. These next examples are also shown in Chapter 9 around how to do shared context. It isn't important to know what that means now, but let's take a look at how `server.ext` is used there. First let's see an onPreResponse event.

```
server.ext('onPreResponse', function (request, reply) {

    var response = request.response;
    if (!response.isBoom) {
        if (response.source && response.source.context) {
            response.source.context.title = "hapi-plugins";
        }
    }

    return reply();
})
```

You can see that we called **server.ext**. Recall in the request lifecycle, the onPreResponse toward the end, right before the response is given. We add a function here, which we add the `title` context and return back the `reply()` object.

The alternative example in Chapter 9 is:

```
server.ext('onRequest', function (request, next) {

    request._sharedContext = {
        title: 'hapi-plugins'
    };

    next();
});
```

This time we are using the **onRequest** part of the request lifecycle. Again we don't really need to know what this does specifically at this point, but recall that **onRequest** is at the beginning part of the lifecycle, so depending on where you need to add your functionality to the process, you have ways to neatly put your logic into the flow. Though not discussed, if you needed to add some custom functionality during the authentication process, you could utilize **onPreAuth** or **onPostAuth**. Keep in mind that these may not always be called in the lifecycle if it isn't relevant.

Summary

Setting up a server is rather simple. A server and plugin are much the same thing. The server can consist of several different plugins. A plugin is just a logical separation of smaller more manageable parts, which can get added to your server instance. We can decorate the server with functions and the server can be configured using JSON configuration files.

Using glue can really make our setup a lot simpler, and using configuration files with rejoice and confidence is a good way to go if there are development and production setups.

Next, you will learn all about routes for our hapi server.

Routes 3

In most places, the term **route** is associated with a certain path you can take to get to your destination. When driving from point A to B, for instance, you may have the option of several different routes. A route is a very specific path between the two points.

In hapi and other frameworks, a route is a specific path that a request takes. On a website, the number of characters you can write after the address **hapi-plugins.com** are only limited to the number of characters your browser will support. But in order to send a request and actually get a response for what you're looking for, you need to know the route of where to send the request. The query then travels through a known path within the framework, and a response is returned back based on several parameters as part of the request. The actual route you've told the query to take is key for knowing how to handle this request. It's the server's first indication of what the client is expecting it to do with the request.

In its simplest form, a route looks like the following:

```
server.route({
    method: 'GET',
    path: '/',
    handler: function (request, reply) {

        return reply({ status: 'OK' });
    }
});
```

This is a great and obvious form for short and simple routes, but when the project gets larger we separate out the behavior to use config instead of supplying the handler like we see here.

We typically store the config in their own file. Before we look at what we've done for this project, we will simplify even further.

In our `lib/routes.js` file, we have the following:

```
var Welcome = require('./controllers/welcome');
server.route({
    method: 'GET',
    path: '/',
    config: Welcome.index
});
```

Then the actual config for the route is in a corresponding file called 'lib/controllers/welcome.js`.

```
modules.export.index = {
    description: 'Show the main page for our welcome page',
    handler: function (request, reply) {

        return reply({ status: 'OK' });
    }
};
```

This keeps the code logically separated, which is typical of a MVC (Model-View-Controller) framework. The logic in the code can get quite extensive, and with this separation, it can easily be organized so that all the logic for a particular route is all in one file. You may decide to go that route, which would be as simple as keeping that particular logic in a file called `lib/controllers/welcome/index.js` instead. Perhaps your terms of service would be in `lib/controllers/welcome/tos.js` under this structure. Of course, there has to be some sense to how large a function is before it gets split out into its own file. But the idea is that the code, when broken up into smaller pieces, is far easier to both manage and read.

Path processing

Routes are unique. Several issues on GitHub have been opened asking about regular expressions, or other types of globbing. It can be difficult to figure out when routes overlap. One of the early design goals of hapi was to ensure that the routing table would be identical each time it's loaded. There should be no surprises. When starting up, hapi will complain about any conflicts and protect you from these types of issues.

How path processing works in hapi is, the router iterates through the routing table on each incoming request and executes the first (and only the first) matching route. Route matching is done on the request path only (excluding query and other URI components). The requests are matched in a deterministic order, so it doesn't matter where you add them. Finally, the routes are sorted from the most specific to the most generic. If you want further details on exactly how that works, see **Path Matching Order**.

Parts of the route

A route object, the argument to `server.route()` consists of just a few easy properties.

method

This determines the HTTP request **method** to be performed on the re-source. The method will be one of the following: GET HEAD POST PUT DELETE TRACE OPTIONS CONNECT PATCH. In practice, it will most likely be one of GET, POST, PUT, DELETE or PATCH, and HEAD is not allowed. hapi allows wildcard methods to be used, which means that when the exact match isn't found, it will use the wildcard instead. The wildcard string is *.

vhost

Specify, this is a virtual host for this route to listen to. A server can be listening to more than one virtual host, but in order for the route to be triggered for one particular host, it can specify the host to listen to. This way, the server can serve up the route depending on the vhost defined. The vhost can be defined as either a string or as an array of strings. The default is to allow any host to use the route.

handler

The handler is a function that returns the output from the route that has been called. It's contingent on the validation and any authentication that precedes it. If the handler is defined via the server, then an object with the property for the name of the handler, as well as any options, can be passed. For a deep dive into the intricacies of the handler, see Chapter 4.

config

If you need additional configuration for your route, you can use the con-fig section to define those. For a simple app, you may not need to specify additional configuration, so this isn't strictly required. However, for more complex configurations, it is better to organize your code under this structure. In this structure, you move your handler to this section so that your configuration is all organized in the same location. An example of a more complex configuration is if you want to add validation or caching.

It is important to note that caching here is different than the server.cache that was discussed in Chapter 2. That functionality caches actual response objects. Caching in this section, is strictly header caching. It will set the Cache-Control header. Below is a trivial example where it will set a cache header for one hour for our /hello route.

```
server.route({
    method: 'GET',
    path: '/hello',
    config: {
            handler: handler,
            cache: {
                expiresIn: 60 * 60 * 1000
            }
        }
});
```

There are so many options in the config section, we feel it's better to refer you to the **documentation**. One that we will cover next, however, is route prerequisites.

ROUTE PREREQUISITES

You may need to initialize a database connection and return it for every single endpoint that you're using. This is a task that's perfectly suitable for route prerequisites. There are of course many other things you could need to set up, but this is probably the most common.

The prerequisite allows you to run any number of functions in both serial and parallel.

The argument for pre is a mixed array. It can contain either other arrays or other objects. Anything that is specified in an array will be executed in parallel, while all the other items are executed in series, e,g:

```
server.route({
    method: 'GET',
    path: '/',
    config: {
        handler: function (request, reply) {

            return reply({ status: 'OK' });
        },
        pre: [
            series,
            series,
            [
                parallel,
                parallel
            ],
            series
        ]
    },
});
```

Each **series** and **parallel** item in the **pre** array are objects with two properties: **method** and **assign**.

```
var dbSetup = function (request, reply) {

    DB.getConnection(function (err, connection) {

        return reply(connection);
    });
};

server.route({
    // ...
    config: {
        pre: [
            { method: dbSetup, assign: 'connection' }
        ],
        handler: function (request, reply) {

            var conn = request.pre.connection;
            conn.exec('select * from blah', function (err,
result) {

                if (err) {
                    var msg = 'DB call failed';
                    return reply(Boom.internal(msg));
                }
```

```
                    return reply(result);
            });
        }
    }
});
```

path

Paths are divided into segments by the / character. That means that anything not part of / is a segment.

It's important to note early that multiple parameters per segment are not allowed.

Because of the hapi rule to always have the routes be in a predictable order, hapi does not support any sort of regular expression syntax because it becomes difficult to tell when paths overlap. But what hapi does allow is using both optional parameters, wildcard parameters and allowing to match multiple segments of a path.

SIMPLE PATH

The named parameterized by parts of the path are indicated by using curly brackets as shown: /fixed/{name}. In the handler, the request object will have a params object. You could utilize the name parameter in the handler with request.params.name. We will cover more details on the request object in Chapter 4.

There are many options for constructing the path. They are later accessed via request.path in the handler, which is also discussed in more detail in Chapter 4.

To illustrate:

```
var internals = {};

server.route({
    method: 'GET',
    path: '/plugins/{name}',
    config: internals.config
});

internals.config = {
    description: 'A path to get info for a specific plugin',
    validate: {
        params: {
            name: Joi.string().required()
```

```
        }
    },
    handler: function (request, reply) {

        var msg = 'The name of the plugin that was passed
  is: ';
        return reply(msg + request.params.name);
    }
};
```

The routes path contains the parameter name which is then checked for validation to be sure it's a string and nothing else. For more on validation, see Chapter 5.

We then access the parameter through request.params to get the name.

OPTIONAL PARAMETERS

In order to specify an optional parameter we use a question mark ?. In regular expressions, this also denotes optional matches and captures so this may already be familiar to you.

   /plugins/{name?}

In this case it may be unclear what to serve up if the name is missing, but you may use it to serve up a list of plugins.

WILDCARDS

If we need to accept any number of segments in order to, for example, proxy a query for a particular route, then a wildcard (*) is a life-saver. Anything using the wildcard character will be stored as an array in the named parameter on the request object. Perhaps if we allowed a query to retrieve any and all results from npm directly we could allow for the path below:

   /npm/{search*}

Because of the nature of the capture here, similar to programming languages that allow any number of arguments to a function (Ecma-Script 6 offers the "rest parameter using ..."), you can only have the rest of the parameter wildcard at the end of a path.

However, if you explicitly define the number of segments that you're allowing on your path, you can put other segments after. In order to define the segments, you add a numeric value after the * to indicate how many you allow.

```
/npm/{search*2}/go
```
The above syntax will capture two segments and store them in the `request.params.search` name as an array.

Server router config options

There are just two options that can be set as part of the server itself.

`stripTrailingSlash` is quite a useful one, but it's set to false by default. The purpose of this route is that if there's a route that looks like `/plugins/like` and the request goes to `/plugins/like/` then there will actually be a 404 error since it didn't match the route. With this option set, the server will strip the trailing slash so that the route will still work.

`isCaseSensitive` defaults to true, which means the routes are case sensitive. It would be poor design to have a route called `/blah` and another called `/Blah` that do different things. This setting means both are treated the same.

Summary

Routes are the path that requests go through in our system. It defines how the requests are handled, and defines how, and the variables we have access to when processing the request. Routes in hapi are unique and have no overlapping possibilities. They are predictable. Routes can be configured with cache settings as well as defined for a specific virtual host (domain name).

Next we're going to look at the handlers that are defined as part of a route.

The handler 4

The handler at its core, is what handles the incoming request for a specific route. It determines how the request will be "handled." The configuration for the route plays a critical part in how the handler needs to behave, and since it's tightly coupled, some configuration for the route needs to be taken into consideration.

When we specify a route for a request, for example, if you're going to download a file from /downloads/<filename> then it is the handler that has all of the logic in it for finding the file in question in order to send it to the connecting client. The handler may also do several other things, like counting how many times the file has been downloaded, access control making sure not just anyone has access to download the file, and so on.

The handler function "handles" all of the decisions and logic between accepting a request from the client and returning a response to the user. hapi has some nice features to offload some work automatically, such as validation. We will look at this in more detail in Chapter 5. All of that work could be done manually in the handler if we ignore this convenience of hapi (why would we dream of doing that though?)

The handler is generally a callback function that is comprised of two arguments: the request and the reply. There are multiple other built-in handlers that we will also go over and discover.

This chapter will cover the various different use-cases for the handler. We're going to delve into the arguments of the handlers and various methods for making life in the handler easier for ourselves.

The request

The **request** object contains all of the information pertaining to the incoming request to the server whether it be from a browser, or some other tool using the API. Since the routing already determines which request will be handled depending on the method, the request received will be limited to whatever is specified. At the end of the day, the full request is available here, which contains the headers and all of the data content sent.

Refer back to the lifecycle of the request to find out how the request travels through the framework.

Attached to the requests is a whole slew of important and useful information that gets used in the handler in order to fulfill a request. In the rest of this section we're going to take a look at how to find this data and what you can do with it.

Bear in mind that there are other functions in the request lifecycle (see Chapter 2) that can add data to the request along the way. We're going to to take a look at a few common ones below.

parameters

Some of the request object data is set as part of direct configuration of the route. For instance, if the route has defined a path that contains an id of a hapi plugin to download, then that will be part of the parameters access on the request object.

```
server.route([
    // ...
    {
        method: 'GET',
        path: '/plugins/{name}',
        config: Controllers.Plugin.get
    }
    // ...
]);
```

The name is the identifier in our case, and this will be accessed via request.params.name. In the above example note we have a GET method. Assuming port 8080, if we did a:

```
curl -XGET http://localhost:8080/plugins/pluginName
```

We'd get the back what is returned in Controllers.Plugin.get. We will be contrasting this with other methods later when we talk about payload.

query

It can be confusing for people new to hapi, what the difference is be-tween a param and a query. The query part of the URL in `https://hapi-plugins.com/search?q=pluginName` is the part after ?. Take a look at the previous example for `/plugins/{name}` to contrast this. The name param was strictly part of the path.

The `request.query` object contains all of the key value pairs that are sent along as a query in the URL.

For example, we could be a bit crazy with the URL to get the informa-tion about a particular plugin on hapi-plugins.com and request some-thing like:

`http://localhost:8080/plugins/blipp?hello=hi`

If we log the output with `console.log(request.query)` then the result we'll see printed to the console would show up as:

```
{ hello: 'hi' }
```

It's worth noting that sometimes the value can be an array. hapi han-dles multiple query keys automatically for you, but you do have to be aware that the result can be a different type than expected.

If instead the URL looks like the following:

```
http://localhost:8080/plugins/blipp?hello=hi&hello=hey
```

We will now see the value as an array:

```
{ hello: [ 'hi', 'hey' ] }
```

payload

request.payload contains information that has been transmitted as part of the request that's not suitable as a query. This may be a file, or a blob of JSON or XML. While it's certainly possible to send payload for all of the request methods (GET, POST, DELETE, PUT, PATCH, etc), it's typically not used for GET. If you do end up seeing payload for GET, you should proba-bly rethink your design.

Let's start out with a simple example for a handler where we'd utilize the POST method of creating a new user.

```
handler: function (request, reply) {

    console.log('name is: ' + request.payload.name);
    console.log('email is: ' + request.payload.email);
    return reply('success');
}
```

If you recall when we talked about params earlier and the GET method, we wanted to contrast this with payload. For the handler above, we could setup a route as below.

```
server.route({
    method: 'POST',
    path: '/user',
    config: {
        handler: handler
    }
});
```

Here you can see the method is POST. In the handler we defined previously, you can refer to your payload with request.payload. In this case the payload has two keys, name and email. We send a POST on the /user path. Once this server was up, in curl we could do something like:

```
curl -XPOST -H "Content-Type: application/json" -d
'{ "name": "Author Name", "email": "author@hapi-
plugins.com" }' https://hapi-plugins.com/user
```

We could also use PUT and it would work the same way.

headers

request.headers is where all of the request headers are stored. Using our previous curl, you would see that in your handler, you could refer to request.headers.Content-Type and that value would be application/json.

The reply

The reply function in the handler serves as a callback and as a way to return control to the framework. The reply function is in charge of replying back to the request to give the result of whatever it is that has been requested.

Reply takes two arguments in order to comply with the regular callback convention where both an err, and result is passed back. In practice only one of the two will be used.

If the first argument is an error object, this will be wrapped in a **Boom** object.

The argument type of reply can be a wide range of different types:

- null
- undefined
- string
- number
- boolean
- Buffer object
- Error object
- Stream object (Stream objects must be compatible with the "streams2" API and not be in objectMode)
- Promise object (hapi's testing uses the bluebird promise lib)
- any other object or array

Organizing handlers

There are many ways to organize code. For simple routes, perhaps it makes sense to throw everything in a route. Here is the simplest example:

```
server.route({
    method: 'GET',
    path: '/',
    handler: function (request, reply) {

        return reply({ status: 'OK' });
    }
});
```

However, when working on large projects, we have found that it can get cluttered to do it this way. This is where we use the route configuration (see Chapter 3) to make life easier for us.

We have organized the code into /lib/routes.js, which is our destination for all of our routes. Whenever we add a new route, or need to see the routes, we have it all in this one simple location. It's a nice convention to follow. It doesn't have to be a routes.js file, since we could also put them in `lib/index.js`. This clearly named file, however, makes it obvious to everyone where it is.

A typical setup has the config for the route living in a completely different file instead, and in that file is where the handler resides.

Our hapi-plugins.com example, has only this in the routes file:

```
server.route([
    {
        method: 'GET',
        path: '/',
        config: Controllers.Home.get
    },
    // ...
]);
```

When architected correctly and the handlers are large, putting each route in their own file can really make the code easier to read. When starting a new route, a file with conventions can simply be copied over and the handler itself modified. It makes for a very clear and easy to read structure.

More discussion on the above example can be found in Chapter 6 if you want more details.

~~Built-in~~ Common handlers

Handlers in hapi 8 were built in. However, hapi 9 which was released shortly after the publication of this book changed to make these handlers plugins instead. The reason behind it was to allow the community faster development on the pieces and also allow for innovation since they're not decoupled from the core.

File and directory handlers are handled by the `inert` plugin. Proxy is handled by the `h2o2` plugin. Views is handled by the `vision` plugin.

In order to use these handlers, simply add them to package.json and make sure they're registered with the server. Plugins themselves will need to use `server.dependency(<plugin>)` in order to make sure they're loaded before the plugin is used.

file

File handler is provided by the **inert** plugin.

File handlers are used to generate static endpoints for serving up files. You are likely to use this with single files that don't fit in the directory handler explained shortly.

We are using the file handler to serve up the favicon, or the little site specific icon that browsers use to associate a website.

We add the favicon to our `lib/routes.js` file as follows:

```
{
    method: 'GET',
    path: '/favicon.ico',
    handler: Controllers.Static.favicon
},
```

There are multiple ways of using the file handler, all of which involve modifying `lib/controllers/handlers/static.js` in our particular setup.

STRING

This is how we're using the handler for hapi-plugins.com and is the most straight-forward approach.

```
exports.favicon = {
    file: __dirname + '/../../public/favicon.ico'
};
```

CALLBACK

A callback takes the request object as an argument that returns the absolute or relative path.

```
exports.favicon = {
    file: function (request) {

        return  __dirname + '/../../public/favicon.ico'
    }
};
```

OBJECT

An object with several options.

```
exports.favicon = {
    file: {
        // 'a path string or function as described above'
        path: __dirname + '/../../public/favicon.ico',
        filename: '??',
        mode: false,
        lookupCompressed: false
    }
};
```

Our path indicates where to find the file to serve up. This can also be set to be the callback function as discussed above.

The filename is an optional filename to specify if spending a "Content-Disposition" header. This defaults to the basename of the path.

Mode specifies whether or not the "Content-Disposition" will be included. By default this is set to false, which means it's not included.

lookupCompressed, if true, looks for the same filename with the '.gz' suffix for a pre-compressed version of the file to serve if the request supports content encoding. It defaults to false.

DIRECTORY

File handler is provided by the **inert** plugin.

A more likely use-case than the file handler is the directory to serve up multiple files. This is common in order to serve files such as images, CSS files or JavaScript files used for the front-end.

Similar to our file handler, the route is set up first in `lib/routes.js` and in this case, we're doing both images and CSS as follows:

```
{ method: 'GET', path: '/css/{path*}', handler:
Controllers.Static.css },
{ method: 'GET', path: '/img/{path*}', handler:
Controllers.Static.img },
{ method: 'GET', path: '/js/{path*}', handler:
Controllers.Static.js },
// ...
```

The handler is defined in a way that's so similar that we're only going to look at the first one as an example:

```
exports.css = {
    directory: {
        path: __dirname + '/../../public/css',
        index: false
```

```
    }
};
```

The path is where the actual data is that we'd like to retrieve and display. There's a number of options that can be set here as well.

We're first and foremost setting index to false. There shouldn't be any need to serve up any index.html in a CSS folder.

The options for directory are as follows:

- **path** - See file handler for an explanation of the various ways of setting this.

- **index** - Can be true, false, or a string representing the name of the index file to look for. The default index file is **index.html** and it is set to true.

- **listing** - Determines whether a directory listing should show in the absence of an index file. Defaults to false.

- **showHidden** - Determines if even hidden files should be displayed in the listing. Defaults to false.

- **redirectToSlash** - If there's a trailing slash, this will be redirected to the path without the slash. Defaults to true.

- **lookupCompressed** - If true, it looks for the same filename with the '.gz' suffix for a pre-compressed version of the file to serve if the request supports content encoding. Defaults to false.

- **defaultExtension** - A string that is appended to file requests if the requested file is not found. Defaults to empty string.

VIEWS

Views handler is provided by the **vision** plugin.

The views handler displays information using templates. In practice, this option isn't very commonly used. The more common approach is configuring the server with the views option, and then using the regular handler with reply.view().

Because hapi supports both, we'll take a brief look at the views handler, and focus more on how to configure the server to directly support views with **reply.view()**.

For our hapi-plugins project, we're not using a views handler, but it should be mentioned how it can be used. This may serve as a case where for whatever reason, the regular server.views needs to be overridden.

In both cases, the server is configured with a views manager.

```
plugin.views({
    engines: {
        html: {
            module: require('handlebars')
        }
    },
    path: __dirname + '/views'
});
```

We're setting the rendering engine and specifying the relative path from which we will be reading the templates. The property in the engines configuration sets the file extension that will be used for that particular rendering engine.

A very basic use-case would look like the following:

```
exports.terms_of_service = {
    view: 'terms_of_service'
}
```

Here view just takes a string with the template filename.

Where we'd want to override the server's views configuration, it would be more elaborate with the view taking an object:

```
exports.terms_of_service = {
    view: {
        template: 'terms_of_service',
        context: {
            serviceType: 'provider'
        }
    }
}
```

For a quick point of clarity, context is the json object with the actual data that is being sent to your template. In this case, in your template terms_of_service you can refer to serviceType in your template and it will fill in the value provider. More discussion on templating is in Chapter 9, and depending on the templating engine, this syntax will difffer.

If there's no context passed to the object above, then it's set to a context object with the following properties:

- payload - containing request.payload
- params - containing request.params
- query - containing request.query

- **pre** - containing request.pre

The view object can also contain an options property, which can serve to override the server view settings.

REGULAR HANDLER USING SERVER.VIEWS

Using reply.view() is the most common way to render a template file. (See section on common handlers and how to register the view function).

For the main page of hapi-plugins, we're rendering just an index file and we're displaying a random quote on the page.

```
module.exports.get = {
    handler: function (request, reply) {

        reply.view('index', {
            finalmsg:
internals.quotes[Math.floor(Math.random()*internals.quotes.length)]
        });
    }
};
```

And in the template we see the following:

```
<div id="finalfrontier" class="col-md-12">
    {{finalmsg}}
</div>
```

If you would like to know more about handlebars, you can read more at: **handlebarsjs.com**.

proxy

Proxy handler is provided by the **h2o2** plugin.

Many times starting out with a proxy can be an easy way to start in on a project. You have some legacy service that you want to replace, and a proxy can be a good way to start. In fact, the proxy feature was the most heavily used feature of hapi. This is precisely how we started to use hapi at WalmartLabs. Below is an example of how you could proxy Google.

```
server.route({
    method: '*',
    path: '/{path*}',
```

```
config: {
    handler: {
        proxy: {
            host: 'google.com',
            port: 80,
            protocol: 'http',
            // 6th redirect get a 300 response
            redirects: 5,
            passThrough: true,
            xforward: true
        }
    }
}
});
```

Here we use a * wildcard for the method. This will match any method that comes in. The path setting simply says to route everything. Finally, in the config section under handler, we have our proxy. You can see we are setting the proxy up for google.com. The redirects setting says that we should only redirect five times as a max. The passThrough setting specifies whether or not to preserve headers on the original request. Finally, the xforward setting tells hapi to add (or append) an 'x-forwarded-for' header to the request.

You can do other powerful things with the proxy handler. You can re-write the request using mapUri, pass local-state from the hapi instance with localStatePassThrough, reject unauthorized requests with rejectUnauthorized, and you can even use a custom function with onResponse to do whatever else you want. Refer to the **documentation** for more details.

Instead of proxying Google, you can proxy your own service here. Proxying is an easy way to get started with something simple. As time permits, you can add routes to your application to take over that downstream functionality. This approach leads to easier troubleshooting due to the smaller change sets.

Adding common methods to the handler

Sometimes there are functions that will need to be accessed multiple times. When that's the case, we can use convenience functions. One way of accessing these is to put all such functions in a common library and draw on them.

hapi, however, has a few other solutions up its sleeve to make this process easier.

Binding to server

Through a binding in the global context, any variable or function can be made available on this within the handler function. This can be useful if you need shared functionality.

The context can be set in a plugin or in the top server level.

We typically use this for some service that we'll need to access throughout the application. Some personal subjective insight can be used when server methods can be used vs the server bind, but in general something that's accessible on the server bind would be something that's initialized for the duration of the app that you don't want initialized each time, as opposed to some convenience function that is self contained.

```
server.bind({
    service: new Service()
});
```

This function will be accessible from any of the handlers as simply this.service(). This can serve as a useful shortcut.

For more information on binding see **hapijs.com/api#serverbind-context**

Decorating the reply

Similar to server.bind this function lends itself to use reply. Decorate is more narrow in the scope that it can be used, but it's perfect for canned replies.

```
server.decorate('reply', 'success', function () {

    return this.response({ success: true });
});
```

We have an option to decorate the reply object or the server object and the first argument is where we specify which one. The second argument specifies the name of the method and the third argument is the call back.

In our handler, we can thus simply call:

```
reply.success();
```

This is a very nice shortcut and saves from changing in multiple places if the JSON object returned changes. It's also a nice means to make sure the replies for success are consistent because it eliminates typos.

You can find more about decorating the server object in Chapter 2.

Tails

Certain actions do not require immediate completion. The type of calls may be a background job of some sort, which is not necessary for the return of the page served to the client. It may be a database call for some update, or it may be any number of things. While not necessary to capture this, we are still likely to want to capture this for logging purposes. When the tails are completed for the request, the server emits a `tail` event.

```
server.route({
    method: 'GET',
    path: '/',
    handler: function (request, reply) {

        var publishTail = request.tail('publish the book in
the background for download');

        HapiBook.publishForDownload({ format: 'pdf' },
function (downloadUri) {

            var mail = Mail({ to: user });
            mail.publishNotification(downloadUri, function
() {

                publishTail();
            })
        });

        reply.view('index');
    }
});

server.on('tail', function (request) {

    console.log('all tails completed');
});
```

Defining the handler using server.handler

The handler can be defined directly on the server object. In practice, this is not a way we define handlers in our own code, however, it's included here as a possible alternative. After all, a lot of code depends on preference.

```
var DB = new Database(options);

server.handler('pluginLike', function (route, options) {

    return function (request, reply) {

            options.DB.getPlugin(request.path.id, function
(err, plugin) {

                if (err) {
                    return Boom.internal(err);
                }

                plugin.like(function (err) {

                    if (err) {
                        return reply.fail();
                    }

                    return reply.success();
                });
            };
        }
});

server.route({
    method: 'GET',
    path: '/plugins/like/{id}',
    handler: { pluginLike: { dbHandler: DB } }
});
```

Liking a plugin example

As a larger example, we're going to take a look at what is happening behind the scenes when we like a plugin on the site. Below is the example.

```
module.exports.like = {
    auth: 'session',
```

```
handler: function (request, reply) {

    var pluginName = request.params.name;
    var username = request.auth.credentials.username;

    if (!username) {
        return reply(Boom.unauthorized());
    }

    var getPlugin = function (user, next) {

        DB.plugin.get(pluginName, function (err, plugin)
{

            if (err || !plugin) {
                var msg = 'no such plugin found';
                return next(Boom.notFound(msg));
            }

            return next(null, plugin, user);
        });
    };

    var addLike = function (plugin, user, next) {

        user.like(plugin, function (err) {

            return next(err);
        });
    };

    Async.waterfall([
        getOrCreateUser,
        getPlugin,
        addLike
    ], function (err, result) {

        if (err) {
            return reply(err);
        }
        return reply({success: true});
    });
}
};
```

Uploading files

Being able to directly upload a file to a website is one of the most basic features that we face as developers, however, it's often quite unnecessarily difficult to find out how to do this. This section takes you through how to handle uploading files and some different options you can take with it.

For our website, we will need to be able to upload packages in order to publish them. This allows us to register packages for the plugin site, and the npm becomes optional with the user's credentials.

Let's begin with the view. Templates will be discussed in Chapter 9, so refer to there on how to make the serving up of the upload page suit your needs. For now, let's take a look at the HTML code required to upload a file.

```html
<!DOCTYPE html>
<html>
    <form action="/plugin/upload"
            enctype="multipart/form-data" method="post">
        <p>
        Choose a file for upload:
        <input type="file" name="datafile" size="40">
        </p>
        <div>
            <input type="submit" value="Send">
        </div>
    </form>
</html>
```

This is a generic upload form that will work with whatever back-end system you may have at your disposal. Simply it will make a form POST to /plugin/upload where the payload for the file is named datafile.

On the receiving side we will have to set up our handler to process the data. The code looks like the following:

```javascript
module.exports.postUpload = {
    description: 'Post a file for upload',
    payload:{
        maxBytes: 209715200,
        output:'stream',
        parse: true
    },
    handler: function (request, reply) {
```

```
request.payload.datafile.pipe(FS.createWriteStream("out"));
      reply('yeah, so... done.');
   }
};
```

Recall in the payload section of this chapter, we can utilize the re-quest.payload object for methods such as POST. Notice that we're giving specific options on how to handle payload. A default payload is limited to 1mb. This is to help prevent malicious and/or incompetent users from bringing down your app, and is one of many features that separates hapi from other frameworks that pay less attention to such security features. When users send very large files, the server can run out of memory. This can be used as an attack to take your services down. In this case we have raised the size of the upload to handle larger files by changing the default maxBytes value to something higher and more practical.

Because we're receiving a file, we have chosen to create a **read-Stream** so that we can pipe the output directly to a file, database, or whatever storage method that's preferred. By moving the file's contents straight in chunks from the request into the readstream as we receive them, we avoid needing to store the entire file in our apps memory before storing it somewhere else. This saves precious time and memory.

Although the default for parsing is raw, we have chosen to include it here. This field tells hapi whether the data will need to be processed as gunzipped (compressed) or sent raw. true and gunzip means the file will be processed.

A few mime-types are supported and looking at the "enctype" at our form above, you can see that we're using "multipart/form-data". hapi supports the following:

- 'application/json'
- 'application/x-www-form-urlencoded'
- 'application/octet-stream'
- 'text/*'
- 'multipart/form-data'

In the handler, we create a **writeStream** for the file and pipe the incoming data to it.

Done and done!

Summary

In this chapter, we learned all of the ways you can use handlers to process and return different types of responses. Next, you will see how you can validate inputs and outputs from handlers and save yourself a lot of time dealing with improper data.

Validation 5

--   **https://github.com/hapijs/hapi/issues/
1613#issuecomment-46332030**

Eran mentioned in a tweet being proud of the impact that hapi is having on data validation. And he should be. Being able to validate both your input data and your output data is a big deal, and to actually have this made easy and an integral part of a framework is a big deal. If you're asking why this is a big deal, hopefully it's not because you're a skeptic, and it's because you simply want to know. We're all working with computers that are extremely efficient at handling data. If we end up with the *wrong* data, it doesn't really matter how efficiently your computer handles the work or what calculations it ends up doing. Not only is it important from the perspective of having the correct data, but it's also important for bugs and other errors that arise from not having it; more so in a dynamic language than anything else. Expected a number and got a string? That could be very bad.

The library that is used most often to do validation within hapi is called joi. When the author first saw Eran give a presentation of hapi at WalmartLabs, Eran started the presentation with a song about hapi. In fact, if you look on youtube, you can find just such a presentation (**https://www.youtube.com/watch?v=Recv7vR8ZlA**). The song was the hapi hapi joi joi song. Given that hapi and joi are both in the song, it may give you an idea how Eran feels about quality and making sure that all data is validated and in a state where we're safe to operate on it.

In this chapter, we will cover the various places to do validation with and without joi.

Types of validations

hapi provides validations for the following inputs: `query`, `payload`, `headers` and `params`. Recall that we learned about these in Chapter 4. Additionally, hapi allows us to do validation on the response.

The formats for validation are always the following:

- `true` - no validation is performed. This is the default.
- `false` - no variables are allowed at all for this section
- Joi validation object. This is what we've discussed so far.
- a validation function.

The most typical one that we end up working with is using a joi validation object, and we'll be focusing on that the most. Validation functions can also be used for things which don't fit regular joi validation.

Joi validation

Validation is configured as part of the route options that get passed to a route. Let's say you want to change a password for a user. You want to send a JSON object password to the endpoint, and change the password to the one you specified. The JSON object would look like:

```
{
    "password": "somepass"
}
```

Then you can set up the route to look like this:

```
var routeOptions = {
    validate: {
        params: Joi.object().keys({
            id: Joi.number()
        }),
        payload: Joi.object().required().keys({
            password: Joi.string().min(8).required()
        })
    },
    response: {
        schema: Joi.object().keys({
            success: Joi.boolean().required()
        });
    },
```

```
    handler: handler
};

server.route({
    method: 'POST',
    path: '/user/{id}/password',
    config: routeOptions
});
```

What we see here is pretty typical. This makes sure that the id in the path URL is going to be a numeric value. The `params` keyword is used and in our server.route, the `{id}` gets made into this parameter. Our method in the server route is a POST and this JSON object gets translated to the `payload` object.

You can see that validation is done on the payload. The password passed in the payload is a string of at least eight characters and it is a required field. In addition, we're telling hapi that the response is expected to be a JSON structure with a success value of either **true** or **false**.

You may be asking yourself, why is response not under the `validate` section? The `validate` section is strictly for inputs. This may not be obvious when you first use hapi with joi. Output (the response) validation can be extremely important if you rely on another API for your work. Having output validation gives you confidence that you are getting the right things from it.

As you've seen in our code so far, we like to have everything broken up and are using the config quite extensively. Because the validation schema can get quite long we often put the validation rules in the internals variable.

The internals variable is the place to put all top-level variables in a file. This prevents pollution in that scope. This is especially useful in cases where we have to access the schema in multiple different places to handle the validation. The example below demonstrates this.

```
var internals = {
    pluginSchema: Joi.object().keys({
    });
};

// Get plugin data

exports.get = {
    description: 'gets plugin data for a specific plugin id',
    response: {
        schema: internals.pluginSchema
```

```
        },
        handler: function (request, reply) {
            // ...
        }
    };
```

Validation for hapi-plugins.com

Let's take a look at the search function for hapi-plugins.com.

```
module.exports.search = {
    validate: {
        query: {
            q: Joi.string().required(),
            sort: Joi.string().optional(),
            fields: Joi.string().optional()
        }
    },
    response: {
        schema: Joi.array().includes(Joi.object().keys({
            name: Joi.string().required(),
            authors: Joi.array(),
            keywords: Joi.array(),
            dependencies: Joi.array(),
            dependents: Joi.array(),
            homepage: Joi.string().allow(''),
            version: Joi.string(),
            license: Joi.string(),
            description: Joi.string(),
        }))
    },
    handler: function (request, reply) {

        var query = null;
        var sort = null;
        if (request.query.q) {
            query = Xss(request.query.q);
        }
        if (request.query.sort) {
            sort = Xss(request.query.sort);
        }
        DB.plugin.search(query, sort, function (err, results)
{

            var converted =  internals.convert(results);
            return reply(converted);
        });
```

```
    }
};
```

You can see here that input validation is being done on `query`. It is expecting three inputs to be strings. One of these q, is the only required input. The additional `sort` and `fields` inputs are optional. However, if they are provided, they must be a valid string. If the request to the API fails to give this, then the error for the front-end will be very obvious and makes it easy to debug for the consumer.

You may notice that `Xss` is used. This is explained in more detail in Chapter 12, but it helps prevent cross site scripting attacks.

Another important thing to notice with this example, is that for `homepage` you can see that for strings, an `allow('')` is added. By default, strings aren't allowed to be empty. This may be annoying for some, but it is better to err on the side of caution when it comes to validation.

You will also notice that there is validation on the response. A schema is provided for what each of these values should be. We have chosen to not separate it out since it is small and easier to read together.

For hapi-plugins.com, once the results are returned from the database, they are converted to an output format where all extraneous data is removed and converted to only what is needed. This data is then validated through this response schema, which is making sure that each item in the array is meeting the expected results.

We can sleep peacefully at night.

Generic data validation with joi

Not only do we use joi validation for validating inputs and outputs, we also use it internally for verifying all kinds of other data. Let's say we're making a call to an external service, or even just to the database. While our data is hopefully not polluted with partial data that gives errors, it never hurts to be careful and validate the data if you're relying on it somewhere downstream.

So we're not covering all the use cases with our validation with hapi-plugins.com and there is a lot more to joi than what we've seen so far. We'll dedicate some more time here to look at what else joi has to offer.

One property that should be remembered is that joi is chainable, which means that you can create shortcuts for yourself.

So imagine you are validating a specific string, maybe an email `Joi.string().email()` or something more complicated that's a longer string.

You could, for instance, assign email to a shorter variable:

`var email = Joi.string().email()` and use this everywhere instead of the longer version.

The author was working on lists: wish lists, wedding registries, baby registries, etc., and had to make sure a proper list type was being sent each time. This is the validation which was used:

```
Joi.string().insensitive().required().valid(['BR', 'SFL',
'WR', 'WL']),
```

In this case we're not caring about the case but we did care that the string needs to be one of the four different list types. Otherwise it was invalid.

Using a validation function

While joi is the heart of validation for hapi validation, it's perfectly possible to do validation without joi. Instead of using the joi signature for the route option for the specific section we want validated, we instead use a validation function.

The function accepts three arguments, `value`, the value to be validated, `options`, the server validation options, and a callback function with the signature `callback(err, value)`

```
var internals = {};

internals.validationFunction = function (value, options,
next) {

    //do something
};


var routeOptions = {
    validate: {
        payload: internals.validationFunction
    }
};
```

Summary

So far, you have gotten an overview of what data validation is, how to use it, and how hapi-plugins.com uses it. There is a wide variety of data types that joi supports, and we recommend you check out the **documentation** for more details. It should be noted that joi does not have to be used specifically for hapi projects. While `validate` is conveniently baked into hapi, joi can be used in other frameworks. Next, you will see how hapi's plugin architecture can enable one application to become more than just the sum of its parts.

Plugins 6

Now that we understand how to validate our inputs and outputs, next we want to talk about how to utilize plugins in hapi to better manage our code. Releasing software as monolithic pieces of code is no better than writing functions that span thousands of lines of code. By writing software as smaller functions that serve a specific role, we can test the functions easier, we can debug things easier, and it's easier to understand the architecture. Plugins follow this model as well, but they are oriented towards functionality of the main software instead of being snippets of code. Plugins allow you to extend current functionality, yet they have the code compartmentalized to divide it and make it easier to maintain and test.

The benefits of splitting code into plugins reaches beyond just your own code, but easily allows users to share code that is beneficial to everybody. For example, you may have written code specific to Facebook authentication (bell) or a plugin to do something as simple as displaying the routes on startup (blipp).

In this chapter we're going to explore how to write a plugin and how to organize your code around it. In addition, we're going to take a look at some of the more popular plugins that we use, as well as the plugins that used to be part of the core project.

A benefit of the plugin model and having replaceable parts in hapi is that you're not bound to a particular way of doing things. If there later comes along a better plugin than the one you're currently using, then switching it out is far easier than if that part of the code is tightly coupled with the code you want to keep. This applies not just to third-party plugins but anything within your own system as well.

When large companies work on plugins across multiple teams, things like caching can be determined on a per-plugin basis. The teams don't have to communicate with each other, and even though the plugins run as part of the same server, routes in the different servers can be configured via the plugin to use, for example, different caching mechanisms that are suitable for what that particular piece of code is doing.

Creating your own plugin

Note how everything in our hapi-plugins project is designed to be a plugin. We have plugins for the router and we have plugins for the models. Even authentication is a plugin.

Let's start by taking a look at our lib/index.js file where all of our plugins are being loaded.

```
server.register([
    Bell,
    Blipp,
    HapiAuthCookie,
    Authentication,
    Controllers,
    Models,
    Routes
],
function (err) {

    if (err) {
        console.log('server.register err:', err);
        return callback(err);
    }

    server.start(function () {

        console.log('server started on port: ',
server.info.port);
        return callback(null, server);
    });
});
```

Anyone using Async may recognize this pattern, since it allows you to easily run many functions. We're big fans of using async methods and this pattern here is very similar. Internally, hapi uses **items**, which are bare-bones async methods to accomplish its goals.

The register functions signature is server.register(plugins, [options], callback).

There are a few different ways to pass plugins, but the one shown here is usually how all of our projects are organized, and we have many. The best part about using the register function way of passing the plugins is that they can easily be made into their own separate npm packages that can be loaded. They can also be shared as their own repositories in github.

When there are many people working together on a bigger project, we have found it to be helpful to split specific components into their own repositories. For example, if you have a blogging system, you could put all routes that have to do with dealing with posts as their own plugin, and all the routes that deal with comments as their plugin as well. Then you have separate owners for each individual piece and this tends to lead to less conflicts in the code. This may not always work well. For example, you may have tightly coupled services. You are the expert when it comes to your own code. It's up to you to decide what's best for your project, and hapi is flexible so you can organize your project how you prefer.

Another separation for code can be to keep your controllers slim and put as much logic into models as possible. They can in turn have their own libraries with the code in them.

With the code separated into smaller atomic parts, code reuse becomes far easier. It is also easier to understanding the architecture. As an example, you may find that you wish some of your testing setup was easier to access between the project. You may end up doing what we did, which was creating another repository just for common testing. This is a very nice approach even within a project but can also be reused across multiple projects.

Let's take a look at one of the pieces in detail by looking at how our handlers are loaded.

```
var load = function (options, callback) {

    options = options || {};
    options.extension = options.extension || '.js';
    var controllers = {};

    var files = glob.sync('*' + options.extension, {cwd:
options.path || __dirname});
    for(var i in files) {
        if (files[i] != path.basename(__filename)) {
            var key = path.basename(files[i],
options.extension);
            key = key.charAt(0).toUpperCase() + key.slice(1);

            controllers[key] = require((options.path ||
__dirname) + '/' + files[i]);
        }
```

```
    }

    if (callback) {
        return callback(null, controllers);
    }

    return controllers;
};

exports.register = function (plugin, options, next) {

    load({path: __dirname + '/handlers'}, function (err,
handlers) {
        if (err) {
            throw err;
        }

        if (process.env.DEV) {
            console.log('handlers:');
        }
        plugin.expose('handlers', handlers);
        next();
    });
};

exports.register.attributes = {
        pkg: require('./package.json')
};
```

We begin with a convenience function called load(). The purpose of load is to go through all of the files in a given directory and require those files. In addition, we're exposing the required handler files under the handler name. These then are used in our lib/handlers.js file to access the handlers for the routes.

The plugin object that's sent to the register function is nothing else than the server object itself. Because of the context it's referred to as plugin here.

The plugin.expose is a function to make the plugin available to the server object via server.plugins[name]. In this particular case it's not likely needed since we're only going to use the handlers in the routes file, however it's good practice to expose the plugins so they can be used anywhere in the application.

The plugin is also getting some attributes set to it. Typically this can just be set to the package.json, but if you want to keep it minimal, or for some reason don't want to use the package.json, then you can just set it with a object that has the name and version properties:

```
exports.register.attributes = {
    name: 'handlers',
    version: '1.0.0'
};
```

This is all there is to most of the plugins. There are a few more things to say about plugins that we use, however.

In addition to expose, we also tend to use `plugin.dependency` as well as `plugin.bind`.

Let's for example say that you're relying on another third-party plugin for some setup that you're doing in your own plugin. This is where `plugin.dependency` comes into play. The dependencies are checked on a per-connection basis. So even if you have the dependencies loaded for plugins on one connection, if you don't have it on the other connection where it's used, hapi will throw an error: `Plugin *api* missing dependency controllers in connection: http://0.0.0.0:8088`.

`plugin.bind` is used when we want to be able to access some piece of data throughout the application but we don't want to keep loading it. This can be initializing or instantiating some piece of data and we only need to do it that one time, perhaps setting up a session, or something else specific to the whole lifecycle of the app.

Our `lib/routes.js` has examples of both use-cases.

```
plugin.dependency('controllers');
plugin.dependency('models');

var Controllers = plugin.plugins.controllers.handlers;
var Models = plugin.plugins.models.models;
plugin.bind({
    models: Models
});
```

The routes file requires the controllers to be set up first since they contain the handlers that the routes use. The models will be used in the plugins route. In addition, because of the bind, the database models will now be accessible anywhere in the handlers as simple `this.models`.

Plugin configuration

Previously, you may not have noticed but there was an options argument that was passed when registering a plugin via the `register` function. To show you again:

```
exports.register = function (plugin, options, next) {

    load({path: __dirname + '/handlers'}, function (err,
handlers) {
        if (err) {
            throw err;
        }

        if (process.env.DEV) {
            console.log('handlers:');
        }
        plugin.expose('handlers', handlers);
        next();
    });
};
```

You can see that options wasn't used anywhere. However, `options` can be used to configure the plugin. Let's suppose we wanted to pass some options for the blipp plugin. Recall this plugin just lists the routes on startup. While routes don't currently support this, it's conceivable that you wouldn't want blipp to actually print the routes table in colors on startup, so you may want to pass it a flag saying to always just print without ANSI colors.

We should be able to see something like the following instead of our original code:

```
server.register([
    Bell,
    { register: Blipp, options: { colors: false }},
    HapiAuthCookie,
    Authentication,
    Controllers,
    Models,
    Routes
],
function (err) {

    if (err) {
        console.log('server.register err:', err);
        return callback(err);
```

```
    }

    server.start(function () {

        console.log('server started on port: ',
server.info.port);
        return callback(null, server);
    });
});
```

The above code is for our entire server instance. The actual blipp plugin would have a register function that would would look like the following:

```
exports.register = function (server, options, next) {

    if (options.color === true) {
        // do colors
    }
    else {
        // turn off colors
    }
    // ...
}
```

In our server startup, we had `options` set to `{ colors: false }`. We pass these options to the plugin, and now the plugin knows to turn off the colors. We saw options being passed back in Chapter 2. If you look in the rejoice and glue areas, you will see how options for the plugins are being passed to the plugin. An example of this was the `opsInterval` in the good plugin area. You can configure your options right in `confidence` and even have different options settings per environment. This allows you to again keep things all in one location so things are easier to manage.

A word on labels and selecting plugins

During registration, plugins can be loaded on specifically designated connections for the server. This is a really important feature of hapi. It allows for the handling of multiple distinct servers as part of one package. The API can be separated from the logic of presenting templates this way.

Actually debugging the setup and making sure the right plugins are registered on the correct server can be a bit of a challenge. We recommend the `blipp` plugin in order to see what's going on in the routing table when loading the server.

```
server.register([
    // plugins ...
    ], { select: 'http' },
    function (err) {

        if (err) {
            console.log('server.register err:', err);
        }

        server.register([
            // plugins ...
            ], { select: 'api' },
            function (err) {

                if (err) {
                console.log('server.register err:', err);
                }

                server.start(function () {

                    console.log('server started on port: ',
server.info.port);
                    return callback(null, server);
                });
            });
    }
);
```

When to use a plugin

The goal was to better manage your code -- EH

We've already touched on some cases of when to use a plugin, but let's go over them again and be more specific. Using plugins correctly can help you architect your code well.

You'll want to create a plugin if there's anything that you can do to separate the work from the rest and reuse across different projects. You may have started looking at the various plugins available for a project, and not found one that suits your needs. It's possible then to create your own plugin. One of the authors found that unlike popular frameworks such as Ruby on Rails, there was no way to have hapi list the different routes that were available upon the start of the application. A plugin was created just to show that simple information.

A project may be, as mentioned earlier, also organized based on the routes available. A plugin may be completely dedicated to serving up only the routes for a specific path. For example, we may have all of the routes for the plugins in one plugin.

```
plugin.route([
    { method: 'GET',  path: '/plugins/upload', config:
Controllers.Plugin.getUpload },
    { method: 'POST', path: '/plugins/upload', config:
Controllers.Plugin.postUpload },
    { method: 'GET',  path: '/plugins/{name}/download',
config: Controllers.Plugin.download }
])
```

And we may have another plugin to handle user information.

```
plugin.route([
    { method: 'GET',  path: '/user', config:
Controllers.User.get },
    { method: 'PUT',  path: '/user/profile', config:
Controllers.User.updateProfile }
])
```

This will make more sense if you have a large project and you need to divide up the work because routes take a lot of logic.

The hapi plugin ecosystem: some common plugins

Let's look at some of the popular plugins in the hapi ecosystem. You can find more plugins on hapi-plugins.com (of course) but we've taken the liberty here to show some of the major ones.

inert

This plugin handles static files. It decorates the reply interface as well as adding both directory and file handlers. See the routes chapter for more information on these handlers as they're described in more details there.

vision

This plugin handles template rendering. It decorates the server and reply interface with a additional functions.

server is decorated `views` and `render` functions to initialize the views manager and `render` allows for template rendering using the views manager.

The `reply` interface is decorated with `view` to render the template according to the manager.

See the routes chapter for more information on this handlers as they're described in more details there.

h2o2

This plugin handles static files. It decorates the reply interface as well as adding both directory and file handlers. See the routes chapter for more information on these handlers as they're described in more details there.

hapi-auth-basic

This plugin provides basic authentication for logging into the application, or just basic authentication in general. Most web-based systems require some form of authentication to gain access to the data. Many frameworks as part of the framework, but by using this modular approach, any authentication form is possible.

More information on hapi-auth-basic is provided in Chapter 7.

blipp

While **blipp** isn't a core plugin, it's nevertheless very useful. It simply displays the routes and the server:port combination when the hapi server is started. It gives a very quick indication of what routes are available and that they're available on the correct server connection.

bell

Bell is much like hapi-auth-basic except that it's using third-party logins such as Facebook, GitHub, Google, Instagram, LinkedIn, Twitter, Yahoo, Foursquare, VK, ArcGIS Online and Windows Live. If you're looking to support logins for those, this is the plugin to use. Third-party plugins are getting added continually. Bell is usually used with hapi-auth-cookie so that isn't explicitly called out on its own.

More information on bell and hapi-auth-cookie is provided in Chapter 7.

good

If you're running a service in production, you'd almost certainly want to use **good**. You get to see how your service is performing with CPU usage, memory, etc. There are many reporters you can use with this program, you can have reports sent to a file logger, to console, or any custom program you write your own reporter for.

More information on good is provided in Chapter 11.

tv

TV is an interactive module used for debugging. It becomes easy to see what requests are received by your service and what it does to handle it.

More information on tv is provided in Chapter 11.

lout / hapi-swagger

Lout and **hapi-swagger** are documentation tools for your routes and setup. It provides api documentation for you, so you don't have to. This can save you some serious time for something that you need to have anyway.

poop

In line with hapi's goal of being silly, **poop** is a plugin for doing a process dump on exceptions. It provides a heapdump (**https://www.npmjs.com/package/heapdump**) and a log file will also be provided containing additional details for debugging.

More plugins

You can find a large list of plugins at **hapijs.com** under `Plugins`.

Summary

Often hapi plugins started as being part of the core project. As the project grew, many sections of hapi were broken into their own plugins. This happened for a variety of reasons. It helps keep things small and manageable. It can be useful to reuse for other applications. It can also be useful to separate out responsibilities between large teams.

Writing plugins can also drive the design in hapi applications. They keep it easy to manage the application and allow for configuration-driven servers. We've shown you how useful they are and how to use options to keep your configurations manageable and flexible.

Next, we will utilize some of the hapi authentication plugins described above and explain how to utilize hapi for your authentication needs.

Authentication 7

From the beginning, authentication has been front and center in hapi. A robust application framework must consider authentication for any useful adoption to take place. There are a large number of authentication strategies that now exist for hapi. One of the nice things about the approach that hapi takes to authentication is that while it's central to the framework itself, the strategies are expected to be provided by external modules. Even to support basic authentication, an external module needs to be installed. As a result, there are many options, some competing, which are available to hapi developers.

Chapter Overview

The following chapter will cover many details on authentication in hapi. Specifically, the following plugins will be covered.

- hapi-auth-basic
- hapi-auth-cookie
- bell (with hapi-auth-cookie)

Scheme vs strategy

It can be a bit confusing when talking about authentication on what the difference is between a scheme and a strategy.

You can think of a scheme as a general auth type like basic or digest. A strategy is a pre-configured and named instance of the scheme. Another way to think about it is an authentication strategy sets up *how* to authenticate technically/mechanically. The strategy can be third party OAuth strategy, a db, cookies, basic, or any custom one you can think of. These rely on an authentication scheme. An authentication scheme sets up *who* is authenticating. The scheme could bet an administrator, user, or custom thing.

Coming up, we will talk about the `hapi-auth-basic` plugin. The strategy for this is simple and it uses the basic scheme to implement this. It is simple because it is just a simple object. When you register the `hapi-auth-basic` plugin, it creates a scheme with the name of `basic`. This is done with the `server.auth.scheme()` method. Once the `hapi-auth-basic` plugin has been registered, you use the `server.auth.strategy()` function to create a strategy with the name of simple, which refers to our scheme named basic. Finally, you tell a route to use the strategy named simple for authentication.

As you go through this chapter and see specific examples, these concepts should make more sense.

hapi-auth-basic

The next step up from a hard-coded username and password is basic authentication. It's not much more secure than a username and password being passed in the clear, but it does serve a purpose for some internal applications. Aside from any usefulness that may or may not exist, it does make for a simple starting point in understanding hapi authentication.

In the early days of hapi, the basic authentication scheme was baked into the module itself. In Chapter 6, we discussed that hapi has evolved and as authentication grew, so did the need to split hapi up into plugins. You will need to install the `hapi-auth-basic` plugin in order to get any basic authentication support in hapi.

For any authentication support to exist in hapi, you must first have a scheme registered with the server. The scheme is the heart of the authentication that will take place. In the case of `hapi-auth-basic` the scheme is registered when the plugin itself is registered.

The only thing left to do is to declare an authentication strategy that will use the scheme. It will become more obvious later, when bell is discussed, but strategies help hapi be an extremely flexible framework because it can support multiple strategies.

Below demonstrates how to register the `hapi-auth-basic` plugin and set it up as a strategy.

```
var Hapi = require('hapi');
var Basic = require('hapi-auth-basic');
```

```
var server = new Hapi.Server();
server.connection({ port: 3000 });

server.register(Basic, function (err) {

    server.auth.strategy('simple', 'basic', { validateFunc:
validate });
});
```

After an authentication strategy is in place, it can be used by individual routes that expect authentication. If you expect all routes to have a certain strategy, you can pass an option when declaring the strategy for mode and set the mode to required.

Another option is to use try, which means to try to authenticate if credentials are provided, otherwise continue to executing the route lifecycle.

A third option exists, named optional, which means that if authentication is attempted and fails the request fails. In the case of basic authentication, the username is passed in the clear, as is. However, the password is expected to be base64 encoded and validated this way. In the previous example, the validate function was missing, as well as the base64 encoding of the password. A more complete set of code is provided below.

```
var Bcrypt = require('bcrypt');
var Hapi = require('hapi');
var Basic = require('hapi-auth-basic');

var server = new Hapi.Server();
server.connection({ port: 3000 });

var users = {
    molly: {
        username: 'molly',
        password: '$2a
$10$iqJSHD.BGr0E2IxQwYgJmeP3NvhPrXAeLSaGCj6IR/XU5QtjVu5Tm',
        name: 'Molly Ringwald',
        id: '2133d32a'
    }
};

var validate = function (username, password, callback) {

    var user = users[username];
    if (!user) {
```

```
        return callback(null, false);
    }

    Bcrypt.compare(password, user.password, function (err,
isValid) {

        callback(err, isValid, { id: user.id, name:
user.name });
    });
};

server.register(Basic, function (err) {

    server.auth.strategy('sobasic', 'basic', { validateFunc:
validate });
    server.route({
        method: 'GET',
        path: '/',
        config: {
            auth: 'sobasic',
            handler: function (request, reply) {

                reply('hello, ' +
request.auth.credentials.name);
            }
        }
    });

    server.start(function () {

        console.log('server running');
    });
});
```

The code above demonstrates how you add a route that expects authentication by passing the strategy name to the route config auth property. You can see that the bcrypt library has a compare function, which will tell us if it is a valid password or not. Because bcrypt is being used here, you can see passwords aren't stored in plain text. That's definitely an improvement.

hapi-auth-cookie

A common authentication scheme of websites is to use cookies to store a security token. Similar to how the basic authentication scheme depends on the developer implementing a `validate` function, the cookie authentication expects the same function. Cookie authentication is provided by the module `hapi-auth-cookie`. The module options support many properties that relate to how cookies are stored, for example a time to live or secure flag property. One of the major differences between cookie authentication and the basic authentication strategies is that the cookie authentication strategy decorates the `request.auth.session` object with properties for setting or clearing session properties. Below is a demonstration of a full application that uses the cookie authentication strategy and registers it on a route that expects authentication.

```
var Hapi = require('hapi');

var users = {
    john: {
        id: 'molly',
        password: 'breakfast',
        name: 'Molly Ringwald'
    }
};

var home = function (request, reply) {

    reply('<html><head><title>Login page</title></head><body><h3>Welcome '
        + request.auth.credentials.name
        + '!</h3><br/><form method="get" action="/logout">'
        + '<input type="submit" value="Logout">'
        + '</form></body></html>');
};

var login = function (request, reply) {

    if (request.auth.isAuthenticated) {
        return reply.redirect('/');
    }

    var message = '';
    var account = null;

    if (request.method === 'post') {

        if (!request.payload.username ||
            !request.payload.password) {
```

```
                    message = 'Missing username or password';
            }
            else {
                account = users[request.payload.username];
                if (!account ||
                    account.password !==
request.payload.password) {

                        message = 'Invalid username or password';
                }
            }
        }

        if (request.method === 'get' ||
            message) {

            return reply('<html><head><title>Login page</title></
head><body>'
                + (message ? '<h3>' + message + '</h3><br/>' :
'')
                + '<form method="post" action="/login">'
                + 'Username: <input type="text"
name="username"><br>'
                + 'Password: <input type="password"
name="password"><br/>'
                + '<input type="submit" value="Login"></form></
body></html>');
        }

        request.auth.session.set(account);
        return reply.redirect('/');
};

var logout = function (request, reply) {

        request.auth.session.clear();
        return reply.redirect('/');
};
```

We have our basic functions setup above. We setup a user. We provided a **login** function which handles what to do when the user submits their username and password. It returns with a message if there is an invalid username or an invalid password. Finally, if everything is fine, it sets a cookie via the **request.auth.session.set** function. A **logout** function is provided that clears the cookie and then redirects back to the main page. Lastly, we have a home function that simply shows a form if they haven't logged in yet. Now to setup the server, and register the plugin.

```
var server = new Hapi.Server();
server.connection({ port: 8000 });

server.register(require('hapi-auth-cookie'), function (err) {

    server.auth.strategy('session', 'cookie', {
        password: 'secret',
        cookie: 'sid-example',
        redirectTo: '/login',
        isSecure: false
    });
});
```

That wasn't too bad. We setup a cookie name and a password and tell it what the redirectTo path is. The last piece is to setup routes.

```
server.route([
    {
        method: 'GET',
        path: '/',
        config: {
            handler: home,
            auth: 'session'
        }
    },
    {
        method: ['GET', 'POST'],
        path: '/login',
        config: {
            handler: login,
            auth: {
                mode: 'try',
                strategy: 'session'
            },
            plugins: {
                'hapi-auth-cookie': {
                    redirectTo: false
                }
            }
        }
    },
    {
        method: 'GET',
        path: '/logout',
```

```
            config: {
                handler: logout,
                auth: 'session'
            }
        }
]);

server.start(function(){
    console.log('server started');
});
```

After starting the server and navigating to the home page at `http://localhost:8000/` you are greeted with a login prompt, as shown below. Entering the username and password "molly" and "breakfast" will log you in. Subsequent requests will result in a message that reads "Welcome Molly Ringwald!". If you logout, the cookie is deleted and the session is cleared. As a result, the next request to the home page will result in showing the login prompt as seen below. For simplicity sake, we didn't use `bcrypt` this time.

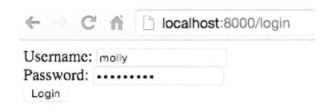

It is important to note that it might be tempting to try to use this for cookies in general. For security reasons, it is important that you keep your session cookies for login and logout separate from your other cookies. If you want to add other cookies to your application, check out the **yar** plugin.

bell

Now that we are armed with hapi-auth-cookie, we could get more fancy if we wanted to have our application use OAuth. We have not done that for our hapi-plugins.com site, but we can walk through a similiar example. We can combine what we learned with hapi-auth-cookie with `bell` to show how you can use multiple strategies together. For example, you may want to have local users, but enhance the application with OAuth usernames for convenience. The code for accomplishing this starts below.

```
var Hapi = require('hapi');
var AuthCookie = require('hapi-auth-cookie');
var Bell = require('bell');

var publicHandler = function (request, reply) {

    return reply('Everyone can see this...');
};

var privateHandler = function (request, reply) {

    return reply('Welcome ' + request.auth.credentials.name);
};

var login = function (request, reply) {

    if (request.auth.isAuthenticated) {
        request.auth.session.set({
            name:
request.auth.credentials.profile.displayName
        });
        return reply('Logged in...');
    }

    return reply('Not logged in...');
};

var logout = function (request, reply) {

    request.auth.session.clear();
    return reply('Logged out...');
};
```

The first part of this code establishes our basic functions. You can see there is a publicHandler for content that any anonymous user can see. Typically, anonymous content includes the login page and its assets. The privateHandler is a function which already is authenticated and just tells us what their name is stored as. The login stores the name that we use in the privateHandler, which is put in a profile variable by bell. Lastly, we have the logout function, which clears the session/cookie.

```
// Create server
var server = new Hapi.Server();
server.connection({ port: 8080 });

server.register([AuthCookie, Bell], function (err) {

    // auth options
    var authCookieOptions = {
        password: 'secret',
        cookie: 'cookieName',
        redirectTo: '/login',
        isSecure: false
    };
    var bellAuthOptions = {
        provider: 'github',
        password: 'secret',
        clientId: 'clientId',
        clientSecret: 'clientSecret',
        isSecure: false
    };

    // strategies
    server.auth.strategy('CookieAuth', 'cookieName',
authCookieOptions);
    server.auth.strategy('YourThirdPartyAuth', 'bell',
bellAuthOptions);
});
```

At this point, you have setup a server, a connection, and registered the plugins. Additionally, you setup the strategies for bell and hapi-auth-cookie. In this example, we are showing how to do this for github. You will need to generate the clientId and clientSecret through a github account and provide this information to bell. The last thing to do is provide the routes and start up the server.

```
// routes
server.route({
    method: 'GET',
    path: '/public',
    handler: publicHandler
});
server.route({
    method: 'GET',
    path: '/private',
    handler: privateHandler,
    config: {
        auth: 'YourCookieAuth'
```

```
    }
});
server.route({
    method: 'GET',
    path: '/login',
    handler: login,
    config: {
        auth: 'YourThirdPartyAuth'
    }
});
server.route({
    method: 'GET',
    path: '/logout',
    handler: logout,
    config: {
        auth: 'YourCookieAuth'
    }
});

server.start(function () {

    console.log('Started...');
});
```

You can see here that our logout and private URLs are protected by cookies still. We have a public handler for /public resources, which may be a generic login page like we had in our cookie example. Finally, we have a login page, which goes to the third party authentication site (github) to get a token. Bell does this magic for you and once you have that, the cookie will be generated. You will not need to login again until your session expires. For more details on the specifics of the providers bell supports go to **bell**.

Summary

In this chapter we explored some basic options that are available for authentication with hapi. The basic authentication strategy can be useful for applications that are protected by a firewall and are internally facing. The cookie authentication strategy is likely more useful, especially for building sites that require a session. Combining the cookie authentication strategy with bell gives you a very robust authentication solution. One of the nice things about hapi is that it supports a mix of any of these and other authentication strategies to fit the needs of the application you are building. Whatever the choice is, rest assured that the creators of hapi and the community at large have tested and support many varying types of authentication strategies.

Models 8

pipe it to /dev/null... is it web scale?

-- Humorous video regarding MongoDB

Models provide the backbone for any useful web application. They are responsible for managing data: connecting to sources of data, reading data, creating data, and so on. Decisions regarding data - including database choices, schema design, and index design - all have a huge impact on how an application performs or even behaves.

Data can come from anywhere: from the web, from a database, from a file, or from a service. For our **hapi-plugins** application, we will be focusing on getting our data from the web via HTTP and from a database.

Using HTTP

One popular way to obtain data for an application is to use third party web APIs. Your application may want to connect to Twitter, Facebook, or Google APIs. Most of these services offer RESTful APIs over HTTP or HTTPS. These types of APIs are extremely easy to work with and can be called from any programming language or operating system.

Desired Usage

Prior to coding the hapi-plugins.com application, we analyzed the NPM API and determined that there were eight relevant APIs:

- Getting list of all plugin names
- Getting list of plugins matching an input keyword string
- Getting list of plugins by name
- Getting list of plugins by depended on

- Getting plugin download count by day
- Getting plugin download count by week
- Getting plugin download count by month
- Getting plugin download count by year

From this, we can design our desired JavaScript API as shown below:

```
/* inside a handler: */
var NPMPackages = new this.models.npm.Packages();
NPMPackages.getShortList(callback);
NPMPackages.getByName('hapi', callback);
NPMPackages.getByKeyword('hapijs', callback);
NPMPackages.getDependedUpon('hapi', callback);

var NPMDownloads = new this.models.npm.Downloads();
NPMDownloads.lastDay('hapi', callback);
NPMDownloads.lastWeek('hapi', callback);
NPMDownloads.lastMonth('hapi', callback);
NPMDownloads.lastYear('hapi', callback);
```

NPM Packages

To start, we configure an instantiable model class object NPMPackages.

```
var Hoek = require('hoek');
var Wreck = require('wreck');
var Util = require('util');

var internals = {};
internals._defaults = {};

internals.NpmPackages = function (options) {

    var Packages = function (override) {

        this.options =
Hoek.applyToDefaults(internals._defaults, options || {});
    };

    return Packages;
};

module.exports = internals.NpmPackages;
```

For each model, we want to retain our typical require statements on top. hapi style guides dictate the use of a module-specific internals object that is essentially locally-private (cannot be accessed or read from outside this file). Inside, we can set global options (in the _defaults object) that can be overridden later. This snippet has no defaults yet though.

Then, we define a JavaScript object that will become our model. In this case, we have an outer object (NpmPackages) and an inner object (Packages). By having an outer object, we can pass in instance-specific options to the inner, final object.

Next, before we add our functions, we set aside important configuration variables into defaults.

We know that the shortlist is obtainable from the URL "**https:// skimdb.npmjs.com/registry/_all_docs**" without any additional parameters. But the other search APIs do take parameters. We abstract all the URLs into two parts: the base URL and parameterized URI paths. Therefore, inside the actual request functions, we will concatenate the base URL and URI to generate the final URL. That is why the URIs are functions.

```
var Hoek = require('hoek');
var Wreck = require('wreck');
var Util = require('util');

var internals = {};
internals._defaults = {
    host: 'https://registry.npmjs.org',
    hostShortList: 'https://skimdb.npmjs.com',
    uris: {
        byShortList: function () { return "/registry/
_all_docs"; },
        byName: function (name, version) {

            if (version) {
                return Util.format("/%s/%s", name, version);
            } else {
                return Util.format("/%s", name);
            }
        },
        byKeyword: function (kw) { return Util.format('/-/
_view/byKeyword?startkey=["%s"]&endkey=["%s",
{}]&group_level=3', kw, kw); },
        byDependedUpon: function (kw) { return
Util.format('/-/_view/dependedUpon?
group_level=3&startkey=["%s"]&endkey=["%s",
{}]&skip=0&limit=1000', kw, kw); }
    }
```

```
    };

    internals.NpmPackages = function (options) {

        var Packages = function (override) {

            this.options =
Hoek.applyToDefaults(internals._defaults, options || {});
        };

        return Packages;
    };

    module.exports = internals.NpmPackages;
```

Next, we add a function for calling the shortlist request.

```
// ...
Packages.prototype.getShortList = function (callback) {

    var method = "GET";
    var url = this.options.hostShortList +
this.options.uris.byShortList();
    var options = {
        redirects: 3,
        timeout: 90000,
        rejectUnauthorized: true
    };

    var processResponse = function (err, body) {

        // Leave room in case response modification required
        return callback(err, JSON.parse(body.toString()));
    };

    var readResponse = function (err, res) {

        if (err) {
            return callback(err);
        }

        Wreck.read(res, {json:true}, processResponse);
    };

    var req = Wreck.request(method, url, options,
readResponse);
};
// ...
```

Wreck requires you to specify four elements. It requires an HTTP method, a URL, optional options argument, and a callback method. We generate the URL as described earlier.

We also define two response callback functions. One, readResponse, returns a response object from the request and tells wreck to parse the response as a JSON object. The second, processResponse, is not required but it is helpful to have in case you need to modify the response before passing it on to your business logic in the controllers.

For example, it may be necessary to remove sensitive or secure fields from the object before passing it on to the user. Or the response schema may not match the desired output. In our case, we are okay passing it unchanged.

Finally, we repeat the steps for the remaining API methods:

```
// ...
Packages.prototype.getShortList = function (callback) {

    var method = "GET";
    var url = this.options.hostShortList +
this.options.uris.byShortList();
    var options = {
        redirects: 3,
        timeout: 90000,
        rejectUnauthorized: true
    };

    var processResponse = function (err, body) {

        // Leave room in case response modification required
        return callback(err, body);
    };

    var readResponse = function (err, res) {

        if (err) {
            return callback(err);
        }

        Wreck.read(res, {json:true}, processResponse);
    };

    var req = Wreck.request(method, url, options,
readResponse);
};

Packages.prototype.getByName = function (arg, callback) {
```

```
    var method = "GET";
    var name = arg;
    var version = null;
    if (arg.indexOf('@') >= 0) {
        var args = arg.split('@');
        name = args[0];
        version = args[1];
    }

    var uri = this.options.host +
this.options.uris.byName(name, version);
    var options = {
        redirects: 3,
        timeout: 90000,
        rejectUnauthorized: true
    };

    var processResponse = function (err, body) {

        // Leave room in case response modification required
        return callback(err, body.rows || body);
    };

    var readResponse = function (err, res) {

        if (err) {
            return callback(err);
        }

        Wreck.read(res, {json:true}, processResponse);
    };

    var req = Wreck.request(method, uri, options,
readResponse);
};

Packages.prototype.getByKeyword = function (keyword,
callback) {

    var method = "GET";
    var uri = this.options.host +
this.options.uris.byKeyword(keyword);
    var options = {
        redirects: 3,
        timeout: 30000,
        rejectUnauthorized: true
    };
```

```
    var processResponse = function (err, body) {

        // Leave room in case response modification required
        return callback(err, body);
    };

    var readResponse = function (err, res) {

        if (err) {
            return callback(err);
        }

        Wreck.read(res, {json:true}, processResponse);
    };

    var req = Wreck.request(method, uri, options,
readResponse);
};

Packages.prototype.getDependedUpon = function (keyword,
callback) {

    var method = "GET";
    var uri = this.options.host +
this.options.uris.byDependedUpon(keyword);
    var options = {
        redirects: 3,
        timeout: 30000,
        rejectUnauthorized: true
    };

    var processResponse = function (err, body) {

        // Leave room in case response modification required
        return callback(err, body);
    };

    var readResponse = function (err, res) {

        if (err) {
            return callback(err);
        }

        Wreck.read(res, {json:true}, processResponse);
    };

    var req = Wreck.request(method, uri, options,
readResponse);
};
```

```
// ...
```

NPM Downloads

To start, again, we configure another instantiable model class object NPMDownloads. Following the convention from before, we split the URL into host and parameterized URI functions. We know that all four API functions will basically be the same except for subtle changes to the URI, therefore, we define a shared method getDownloadsBy to be used by the other methods.

The lastYear's URI is slightly more complicated than the rest, since we have calculated date ranges for today and a year prior to today. But it is not that complicated once you break it down.

```
var Hoek = require('hoek');
var Wreck = require('wreck');

var internals = {};

internals._defaults = {
    host: 'https://api.npmjs.org',
    uris: {
        'last-day': function (_module) { return '/downloads/
range/last-day/' + _module; },
        'last-week': function (_module) { return '/downloads/
range/last-week/' + _module; },
        'last-month': function (_module) { return '/
downloads/range/last-month/' + _module; },
        'last-year': function (_module) {

            var today = new Date();
            var from = [today.getFullYear() -
1,today.getMonth + 1, today.getDate].join('-');
            var to = [today.getFullYear(),today.getMonth +
1, today.getDate].join('-');
            var dateRange = [from, to].join(':');
            return '/downloads/range/' + dateRange + "/" +
_module; }
    }
};

internals.NpmDownloads = function (options) {

    this.options = Hoek.applyToDefaults(internals._defaults,
options || {});
```

```
      return this;
};

internals.NpmDownloads.prototype.getDownloadsBy = function
() {};
internals.NpmDownloads.prototype.lastDay = function () {};
internals.NpmDownloads.prototype.lastWeek = function () {};
internals.NpmDownloads.prototype.lastMonth = function () {};
internals.NpmDownloads.prototype.lastYear = function () {};

module.exports = internals.NpmDownloads;
```

Next, we fill out the shared function for calling the downloads request. But unlike the previous functions, this one returns a function that we use to generate the other requests. The other functions basically become wrappers for getDownloadsBy.

```
// ...
internals.NpmDownloads.prototype.getDownloadsBy = function
(_type, range) {

    var self = this;
    return function (moduleName, callback) {

        var method = "GET";
        var uri = self.options.host +
self.options.uris[range](moduleName);
        var options = {
            redirects: 3,
            timeout: 30000,
            rejectUnauthorized: true
        };

        var processResponse = function (err, body) {

            // Leave room in case response modification
    required
            return callback(err, body);
        };

        var readResponse = function (err, res) {

            if (err) {
                return callback(err);
            }

            Wreck.read(res, {json:true}, processResponse);
        };
```

```
        var req = Wreck.request(method, uri, options,
readResponse);
    };
};
// ...
```

Finally, we factor in **getDownloadsBy** for the remaining API methods by configuring only the differences between functions:

```
// ...
internals.NpmDownloads.prototype.lastDay = function
(moduleName, callback) {

    return this.getDownloadsBy('point', 'last-day')
(moduleName, callback);
};

internals.NpmDownloads.prototype.lastWeek = function
(moduleName, callback) {

    return this.getDownloadsBy('point', 'last-week')
(moduleName, callback);
};

internals.NpmDownloads.prototype.lastMonth = function
(moduleName, callback) {

    return this.getDownloadsBy('point', 'last-month')
(moduleName, callback);
};

internals.NpmDownloads.prototype.lastYear = function
(moduleName, callback) {

    return this.getDownloadsBy('point', 'last-year')
(moduleName, callback);
};
// ...
```

PLUGINS MODEL: ACTUAL USAGE

Back in the handler, we want to combine the results between the NPM Package search results with an array of packages. We also want to ensure the list is unique by name. Then, for each unique module, we need to grab the full module data using **getByName**. Finally, we want to take this list and batch add/update to the database.

To ensure uniqueness, we use a library called `lodash` and the `uniq` function. We pass it a list of just module names and it will strip out duplicates. But to start, we need to pull a list of hapi related modules.

```
Async.parallel({
    shortlist: function (cb) { return
NPMPackages.getShortList(cb); },
    hapiKeyword: function (cb){ return
NPMPackages.getByKeyword('hapi', cb); },
    hapijsKeyword: function (cb){ return
NPMPackages.getByKeyword('hapijs', cb); },
    hapidotjsKeyword: function (cb){ return
NPMPackages.getByKeyword('hapi.js', cb); },
}, function (err, results) {
//...
```

As we have seen before, we are using the Async parallel pattern here to request four API calls at the same time and combine the results. This is important since we need the data from all four sources to identify which plugins are hapi related.

```
var hapiKeyword = results.hapiKeyword.rows.map(function
(module){

    return module.key[1];
});

var hapijsKeyword = results.hapijsKeyword.rows.map(function
(module){

    return module.key[1];
});

var hapidotjsKeyword =
results.hapidotjsKeyword.rows.map(function (module){

    return module.key[1];
});
```

Some of the four sources return data in the same format, like the three keyword related calls, so we walk through those results via the map function to convert the responses to a simple array of plugin names. In this case, the name is stored in `module.key[1]` for all three keyword responses.

```
var NameMatchSuffix = /[-]hapi/ig;
var NameMatchPrefix = /hapi[-]/ig;

var shortlist = results.shortlist.rows.filter(function
(module){

    return NameMatchPrefix.exec(module.id) ||
NameMatchSuffix.exec(module.id);
}).map(function (module){

    return module.id;
});
```

The shortlist returns a plain list of all plugin names, so we need to apply a Regular Expression to find only the hapi related plugins. That is what NameMatchPrefix and NameMatchSuffix are doing.

```
// Ensure the list is unique
var plugins =
_.uniq(shortlist.concat(hapiKeyword).concat(hapijsKeyword).concat(hapi
```

Next, the line with _.uniq() is joining all of the module names from the four calls and eliminating duplicates via the lodash's *unique* function. Now, we have a list of all modules that either have hapi- or -hapi in the name or in the keywords.

It is, however, just a list of names. To do anything useful, we need the data associated with each of these modules. So, we use the Async.map function to apply the NPMPackages.getByName function to each of the module names. This will perform all of the individual API calls in parallel and combine the results at the end to generate a list of module data.

```
// Asynchronously apply getPluginData to every element in
plugins
Async.map(plugins, NPMPackages.getByName, function (err,
results){

//...
```

From here, we need to filter out unpublished modules and ultimately return the results (or error(s)).

In order to see the big picture, here is the entire function shown together:

```
var _ = require('lodash');
var NameMatchSuffix = /[-]hapi/ig;
```

```
var NameMatchPrefix = /hapi[-]/ig;
// ...
module.exports.populateReal = {
    handler: function (request, reply) {

        var NPMPackages = new this.models.npm.Packages();
        Async.parallel({
            shortlist: function (cb) { return
NPMPackages.getShortList(cb); },
            hapiKeyword: function (cb){ return
NPMPackages.getByKeyword('hapi', cb); },
            hapijsKeyword: function (cb){ return
NPMPackages.getByKeyword('hapijs', cb); },
            hapidotjsKeyword: function (cb){ return
NPMPackages.getByKeyword('hapi.js', cb); },
        }, function (err, results){

            if (err) {
                throw err; // TODO: replace with boom err
            }

            // Generate lists of keys for each set of search
results

            var shortlist =
results.shortlist.rows.filter(function (module){

                return NameMatchPrefix.exec(module.id) ||
NameMatchSuffix.exec(module.id);
            }).map(function (module){

                return module.id;
            });

            var hapiKeyword =
results.hapiKeyword.rows.map(function (module){

                return module.key[1];
            });
            var hapijsKeyword =
results.hapijsKeyword.rows.map(function (module){

                return module.key[1];
            });
            var hapidotjsKeyword =
results.hapidotjsKeyword.rows.map(function (module){

                return module.key[1];
            });
```

```
                // Ensure the list is unique
                var plugins =
_.uniq(shortlist.concat(hapiKeyword).concat(hapijsKeyword).concat(hapi‹

                // Asynchronously apply getPluginData to every
element in plugins
                Async.map(plugins, NPMPackages.getByName,
function (err, results){

                        if (err) {
                            throw err;
                        }

                        // Ensure unpublished modules are not added
                        results = results.filter(function (result){

                            if
(result.time.hasOwnProperty('unpublished')) {
                                if (new
Date(result.time.unpublished.time) > new
Date(result.time.modified)) {
                                    return false;
                                }
                            }
                            return true;
                        });


                        // Update the database with results
                        DB.plugin.batchCreate(results, function
(err, success) {

                            if (err) {
                                throw err;
                            }
                            return reply("<pre>" +
JSON.stringify(results, null, 2) + "</pre>");
                        });
                    });
                });
        }
};
```

Now you have seen two ways to create Models that make calls to RESTful API endpoints. One was a general way to make requests and the second was to generate wrappers to make requests. It should be easy to adapt any of these examples to accommodate other third-party RESTful APIs in your own projects.

Next up, we'll continue exploring models and how to connect and query a database.

Using a database

In general, developers have complete flexibility when using databases with hapi - any database, any ORM, or any library can be used. hapi does not impose any restrictions whatsoever. You can use one database for one project, another for a second project, or use ten databases for a third project. hapi tries to make developers happy by not getting in the way.

For the **github.com/hapijs-edge/hapi-plugins.com** application, we've selected the popular MongoDB for our database and we will use the Mongoose driver to connect to our database. For information about other database options and why we chose MongoDB, please see the Models section of Chapter 13 Appendix.

Setting up the database

Setting up MongoDB for an application is fairly well documented on **mongodb.org**. However, for rapid development, it is faster to develop locally or to use **Compose** (aka MongoHQ) to generate a free development database instance for you.

Once an instance is set up, a database name has to be created. We have chosen the instance name 'hapi-plugins' and a database name 'hapi-plugins'. If you change these names, remember to replace them in the examples below in the connection string. If you set up authentication using a username and password (like how we have setup in our production database), remember to add that to the connection string.

Collections are lists of documents. Mongoose will create these for you as you use it so it is not necessary to create by hand unless you want to impose size and maximum document limits.

Connecting to the database

Mongoose provides a high level API for connecting the MongoDB instance. It accepts only a mongodb connection string that can contain host, username, password, database, and so on. Subsequent calls and queries to the database are automatically queued until the connection is complete. Therefore, it is not necessary to nest code in an asynchronous block while waiting for the connection to be made.

In the hapi-plugins.com application, we want to connect to a locally running instance of MongoDB while we develop, but then we also want to connect to the production database when deployed. We use environment variables to dictate what environment to run. The Node.js global, process-wide variable `process.env` contains all of the shell environment variables available to our application.

To enable production, we run our application as `PRODUCTION=1 node index.js`.

Note: Production database credentials in this chapter have their passwords removed. Replace these credentials with proper ones for the database that you create.

```
var databases = {
    development: 'mongodb://localhost/hapi_plugins',
    production: 'mongodb://hapi:{{PASSWORD}}@c278.lighthouse.
0.mongolayer.com:10278,c278.lighthouse.1.mongolayer.com:
10278/hapi-plugins?replicaSet=set-54ebe690660d07da1a000f09'
};

if (process.env.PRODUCTION) {
    Mongoose.connect(databases.production);
}
else {
    Mongoose.connect(databases.development);
}
```

Using this pattern, we can easily differentiate our environments. When developing locally, we use a local database. Then, production uses the live, scalable, hosted database.

An alternative pattern is to the include the database connection string itself in the ENV like so:

```
// $ `MONGOSTR='mongodb://localhost/hapi_plugins' node
index.js`
Mongoose.connect(process.env.MONGOSTR);
```

This has the added benefit of not storing your connection string anywhere in your code. This may be extremely important if you plan to open source your code or in the event your application servers become compromised, since hackers would have direct access to your database after reading through the code.

Schema Design

Before we make any queries to the database, it is generally helpful to design a rough schema beforehand. Even though MongoDB does not require or enforce Schemas, our schemas define how your data is structured and can help you enforce data types. It helps to know how you plan to access and use the data first.

For the hapi-plugins.com application, we plan to allow anonymous visitors to:

- Search for plugins by name, description, author, and keyword.
- Log in & manage their plugins
- Add their own plugin to the list
- Like or unlike a plugin

In the background, we also need to be able to:

- Add a plugin to the list
- Remove a plugin from the list

Therefore, we know plugins must have a name, description, author(s), and keywords. NPM already prevents duplicate module names, so we know that names will be unique and thus we can use name as a primary key. Also, we know from looking at NPM that NPM modules also have versions, licenses, repository URLs, homepages, dependencies, dependents, and a bunch of statistics. It also has time information about when the module was created and updated. From this, we can define our first schema for our hapi-plugins application.

```javascript
var internals = {};

internals.plugin = new Mongoose.Schema({
    'name': { type: String, required: true },
    'description': { type: String, required: false },
    'version': { type: String, required: true },
    'authors': { type: Array, required: false },
    'license': { type: String, required: false },
    'repository': { type: String },
    'homepage': { type: String },
    'updated_at': { type: Date, default: Date.now },
    'created_at': { type: Date, default: Date.now },
    'keywords': { type: Array },
    'dependencies': { type: Array },
    'dependents': { type: Array },
    'stats': {
```

```
        'releases': { type: String },
        'downloads': { type: String },
        'downloads_this_month': { type: String },
        'open_issues': { type: String },
        'pull_requests': { type: String }
    }
});

var plugin = Mongoose.model('plugin', internals.plugin);
```

In the above schema, we have defined all of the relevant fields in each document and some data type requirements. In some cases, there are also fallback defaults in case we do not provide a value for these fields on creation.

MongoDB will let us find items quickly on fields that are indexed. If we end up searching something that is not indexed, MongoDB must search through the entire list of documents. Since we must be able to search quickly across different fields, we have to use indexes.

```
// ...
internals.plugin.index({
    name: 1,
    description: 1,
    authors: 1,
    keywords: 1
});
```

Now for users, we know they should have a username, possibly a display name, an email address, create/update timestamps, and a list of likes. Since we're using MongoDB, data should be denormalized (meaning they should be grouped instead of split into separate tables, even if this means repetitions). The plugin "Likes" makes sense to be associated with Users since abstractly each user basically has a list of likes.

```
var internals = {};

internals.user = new Mongoose.Schema({
    'username': { type: String, required: false },
    'name': { type: String, required: false },
    'email': { type: String, required: false },
    'updated_at': { type: Date, default: Date.now },
    'created_at': { type: Date, default: Date.now },
    'likes': [internals.plugin]
});

var user = Mongoose.model('user', internals.user);
```

SEARCHING PLUGINS

The most crucial part of the hapi-plugins.com application is the ability for users to search for plugins. We want the search to be flexible. The visitor may want to search for a plugin by name if they know it. They may only know what a plugin "needs" to do and can search for a keyword or word that may be in the description. Finally, visitors that may know who created the plugin, and so they can search for all plugins made by that author.

The logic for accommodating this is a little complicated. It involves generating a MongoDB query that simultaneously searches the query-string across all of the relevant fields. In the example below, it is generating a MongoDB query object matching our criteria and executing it.

```
internals.plugin.statics.search = function (queryString,
sortString, callback){

    var query = {};
    if (queryString && queryString.length > 0) {
        var pattern = new RegExp(queryString, 'ig');
        query = {
            '$or': [
                {'name': pattern},
                {'description': pattern},
                {'author': pattern},
                {'authors': {
                    '$regex': pattern
                }},
                {'keywords': {
                    '$regex': pattern
                }}
            ]
        };
    }
    var sortOrder = 1;
    var sortBy = sortString || 'name';
    if (sortBy[0] === '-') {
        sortOrder = -1;
        sortBy = sortBy.slice(1);
    }
    var sort = {};
    sort[sortBy] = sortOrder;
    return this.find(query).sort(sort).exec(callback);
};
```

There is a lot going on in the search function above. First, the search function accepts two important arguments and a callback where the results will be sent.

The first is the query made by the user. We take the query and tell the database to match it with all the relevant fields: name, descriptions, author, authors, and keywords.

The second argument determines sort order. When we grab results from the database, it has to know in what order to return (ascending or descending and by what field). We are using the convention of "-name" to mean descending by name and no minus sign, "-", to mean ascending. If sortString is null, we default to name ascending.

We take these two arguments and execute a find query on the database.

Now, back in the controllers, we can define a search handler to use our new database search method. In this handler, we will also validate and sanitize the inputs to make sure no invalid or malicious inputs are entered.

```
module.exports.search = {
    validate: {
        query: {
            q: Joi.string(),
            sort: Joi.string().optional(),
            fields: Joi.string().optional()
        }
    },
    handler: function (request, reply) {

        var query = null;
        var sort = null;
        if (request.query.q) {
            query = Xss(request.query.q);
        }
        if (request.query.sort) {
            sort = Xss(request.query.sort);
        }
        DB.plugin.search(query, sort, function (err, results)
{

            if (err) {
                return reply({status:-1, error:
err}).code(500);
            }
            return reply(JSON.stringify(results, null, 2));
        });
```

```
        }
    };
```

In the above search handler, we set up validation rules on the query parameters like we have shown in Chapter 5 Validation. A new convention shown above involves the Xss module. This module / function sanitizes the inputs by escaping HTML entities and other possibly malicious tricks. You will learn more about this later in Chapter 12 Security.

After the inputs have been validated and sanitized, we pass this request to the model's search function. Inside the callback, if an error is returned, we return a nice JSON error message. But if it is successful, we return a pretty printed JSON response.

And that is how we enable users to search through our plugin repository. But there is nothing in there yet!

ADDING PLUGINS

In order to search plugins, we need a database of actual plugins and their data. Obtaining the list of matching NPM modules was covered previously. For now, we need the ability to add a single plugin to the database.

```
internals.plugin.statics.createOrUpdate = function
(pluginJS, callback) {

    var self = this;
    var pluginObj = internals.pluginJStoObj(pluginJS);
    self.update({ name: pluginObj.name }, pluginObj,
function (err, numberAffected, raw) {

        if (numberAffected === 0) {
            var plugin = new self(pluginObj);
            return plugin.save(callback);
        }

        return callback(err);
    });
};
```

MongoDB behaves differently from other databases. It is safer to add a new plugin via an "Update" to the plugin name's document. This way, if it already exists, it could be updated simultaneously. But if it does not already exist, it will be created.

Also, inside the `createOrUpdate` function, we use a function `internals.pluginJStoObject` that has not yet been defined. We will define this in Chapter 9 Templating, when we receive data from NPM and must map it to our schema.

Additionally, to make things easier as developers, we also add a function for adding batches of plugins asynchronously. Inside this function, we also added a bit of code to prevent unpublished NPM modules from being registered in our database.

```
internals.plugin.statics.batchCreate = function (pluginsJS,
callback) {

    var self = this;
    var addPlugin = function (pluginJS) {

        return function (next) {

            self.createOrUpdate(pluginJS, next);
        };
    };

    var batch = [];

    for (var i = 0, il = pluginsJS.length; i < il; ++i) {
        var pluginJS = pluginsJS[i];
        var unpublished = Hoek.reach(pluginJS,
'time.unpublished');
        if (!unpublished) {
            batch.push(addPlugin(pluginJS));
        }
    }

    Async.parallel(batch, callback);
};
```

This makes it easier to add multiple entries to the database at once instead of calling an add function manually for every entry. Since these database operations typically run over the network, they are truly asynchronous. Therefore, Async.parallel runs in true parallel fashion and can complete this operation very quickly.

Summary

In this chapter, we've learned how to connect to third-party HTTP APIs and deal with database related stuff: define schemas, make queries, and add documents. You can now customize and add your own collections or databases. As mentioned, there is an Appendix with a reference section for examples using the other popular databases in the book. Next up, we will see how to take this data and display it to the user in a human readable way with templating.

Templating 9

In the last chapter (Chapter 8 Models), we saw how easy it was to obtain and store data. Now, we will see how to present the data back to the user.

hapi is primarily intended for building RESTful JSON APIs. However, when working in the web, it is often essential or helpful to respond to HTTP requests with HTML to be rendered by a browser. Since the output responses depend on the input, or on which user requests the data, it is not always possible or ideal to simply hardcode the same response for every response. The best method to customize responses is with templating. In hapi, templates are referred to as views.

In order to use templates and rendering templates in hapi, we need to require the templating plugin **vision**. Prior to hapi 9.0 the views plugin was bundled with hapi core. Now this plugin needs to be registered as part of the server and in any plugins it should be set as a dependency using `server.dependency('vision')`.

hapi supports most templating engines out of the box. This chapter will include working examples for six of the most popular engines: Handlebars.js, Mustache.js, Jade, Dust, eco, and ECT. For an overview on these, please see the Appendix at the end of the book.

In a typical web application, the end-user visits a URL, the URL maps to a handler in a web server, the handler does some business logic to prepare some data, and finally, the web server responds with data to the end-user in HTML format.

There are many different ways to respond with HTML. The two primary methods are concatenation and templating systems.

In the old days of web development, HTML was generated by concatenating or adding HTML strings with variables, sort of like this:

```
var html = '<html><head><title>' +
    page_title +
```

```
    '</title></head><body>' +
    content +
    '</body></html>';
return reply(html);
```

Thankfully, this tedious and inflexible method has gone out of style and has been replaced by modern templating systems. However, this concatenation method is still possible, and some teams may use it for the sake of efficiency in the case of one-line responses.

Meanwhile, with respect to modern web applications, a templating system merges a template responsible for output formatting with data into a consistent format - like HTML.

For example, a Handlebars (or Mustache) template like this:

```
<html>
    <head>
        <title>{{page_title}}</title>
    </head>
    <body>
        {{content}}
    </body>
</html>
```

combined with context data like this:

```
var context = {
    page_title: 'Templating is fun!',
    content: '<h1>Hello world!</h1>'
}
return reply.view('index', context);
```

will return HTML output like this:

```
<html>
    <head>
        <title>Templating is fun!</title>
    </head>
    <body>
        <h1>Hello world!</h1>
    </body>
</html>
```

Using a template, data can quickly be added, moved around, or re-moved entirely. The work can be split up - designers work on templates while developers supply contexts. Templates can easily be swapped out as part of a redesign or conditionally (show user X design if their settings specify a preference; otherwise, Y).

So, a template system is far less tedious and far more flexible to use than the alternative.

Configuration

In hapi, views must be configured before they can be used. Views must know what engine(s) to run and where to find files - those are required. The other options are not required.

Options

When configuring views, there are three main options to configure: engines, compileMode, paths. In the next section, we'll discover the various sub-options you may need to make your views work properly.

ENGINES

The engines configuration object tells views what file extensions to look for and what templating engine should be used.

The engines object expects file extensions (without the dot '.') as keys and templating system compilers as values. The below example ("engines-breakdown.js") would match anyfilename.extension and use the some_compiler engine.

```
engines: {
    "extension": require('some_compiler')
},
/* ... */
```

Using this system, it is possible to mix and match multiple templating systems as long as they all use different file extensions:

```
var Hapi = require('hapi');

var server = new Hapi.Server();
server.views({
    engines: {
        html: require('mu'),
        jade: require('jade'),
        hbs: require('handlebars')
```

```
    },
    defaultExtension: 'hbs',
    path: __dirname + '/views'
});
```

If you do mix and match templating engines for whatever reason, you should be aware of a couple of things. If you want to use the `reply.view('templateName', context)` syntax, it needs to understand what the default extension is. In the above example, you can see how we pick `hbs` as that default extension. This setting isn't required. You can just add the extension like `reply.view('templateName.hbs', context)`. If the file has an extension that isn't your `defaultExtension` then you need to give it that extension.

COMPILEMODE OPTION

The `compileMode` option is used to tell hapi whether to expect a synchronous templating engine or an asynchronous one. hapi expects the engine object to contain a `compile` method that can either be either format, but not both. By default, hapi expects synchronous engines. Here is a synchronous compile function.

```
{
    compile: function (template, options) {

        return function (context, optionsOverride) {

            // return string template integrated with context
        }
    }
}
```

Next we are doing the same thing asynchronously.

```
{
    compile: function (template, options, callback) {

        var error = null;
        return callback(error, function (context,
optionsOverride, internalCallback) {

            var output = ''; /* set with string template
integrated with context */
            return internalCallback(null, output);
        }
```

```
        }
    }
```

Depending on the templating engine, you will see later on that the default compileMode may be need to be overridden to 'async'.

PATHS

hapi views need to know where to look for template files. There are multiple path configurations depending on your project's needs.

- path: points to the main directory where to look for template files
- partialsPath: points to the directory where to look for partials (if the engine supports Partials)
- helpersPath points to directory where template helper functions are defined (if the engine supports Helpers)
- layoutPath: the directory that contains the layout template (usually layout.{extension} or layout.html)
- relativeTo: path used as a prefix to other directories (enables relative paths in the other path settings)

Additionally, there are two potentially important path-related settings:

- allowAbsolutePaths: (boolean) that enables the use of absolute paths in path settings (default: false)
- allowInsecureAccess: (boolean) that enables support for moving up directories (using '../')

The allowInsecureAccess variable should be used with extreme caution. This can potentially enable users to access otherwise secure files on the server's operating system such as password files, files with sensitive data, and more.

GLOBAL VS SPECIFIC

All of the global view settings can be applied to a specific individual templating engine that will override any global settings. This requires moving the compiler object (typically, the result of the require call) to the module key to leave room for additional options. In the below example ("specific-view-settings.js"), the default compileMode has been changed to 'async' but 'html' files will be executed or render using handlebars in synchronous compile mode.

```
engines: {
    compileMode: 'async',
    engines: {
        html: {
            module: require('handlebars'),
            compileMode: 'sync'
        }
    }
    path: '/path'
}
```

MORE OPTIONS

More options are detailed in the **API documentation**.

STARTER EXAMPLES

First let's start out with Mustache.js.

```
var Hapi = require('hapi');

var server = new Hapi.Server();
server.views({
    engines: {
        html: require('mu')
    },
    path: __dirname + '/views'
});
```

This is pretty simple. It's going to look in the views directory for 'html' files. When you call the `request.view('templateName', { context })` type function mentioned previously, it will compile and serve this up to the client. Next let's look at Handlebars.js.

```
var Hapi = require('hapi');

var server = new Hapi.Server();
server.views({
    engines: {
        html: require('handlebars')
    },
    path: __dirname + '/views'
});
```

You can see this example is essentially the same. This should make sense since Handlebars.js is largely compatible with Mustache.js. Next up is jade.

```
var Hapi = require('hapi');

var server = new Hapi.Server();
server.views({
    engines: {
        jade: require('jade')
    },
    path: __dirname + '/views',
    compileOptions: {
        pretty: true
    }
});
```

We need to add an additional setting called compileOptions here and set pretty to true. hapi tries to handle these views in a generic way, and depending on the templating engine, you can see these slight differences. Next up, dust.

```
var Hapi = require('hapi');

var server = new Hapi.Server();
server.views({
    engines: {
        // requires `dustjs-linkedin` to be npm installed
        html: require('hapi-dust')
    },
    path: __dirname + '/views'
});
```

This is pretty straight forward again. There is only an additional note here that you need to have dust-linkedin installed and in your package.json file as a requirement. Finally the most complex example, ECT.

```
var Hapi = require('hapi');
var ECT = require('ect');
var ectRenderer = ECT({
    watch: true,
    root: __dirname + '/views'
});

var server = new Hapi.Server();
server.views({
```

```
engines: {
    ect: {
        compile: function (tmpl, opts) {

            return function (context, engineOptions) {

                return ectRenderer.render(opts.filename,
context);
            }
        },
        compileMode: 'sync'
    }
},
basePath: __dirname,
path: './views'
});
```

You will see quite a bit more is required. We need to help hapi along with how the compiling is done by providing a compile function. Additionally, you need to tell hapi to use sync in the compileMode that was discussed previously in this chapter.

By showing a variety of templating engines, you can more clearly see how hapi handles the differing solutions. You can find additional templating solutions under the Plugins section of the hapijs.com website under **Templating**. If you don't find what you need, open up a discussion or considering helping the community to get this templating engine added.

View Loading

Views are called and loaded from inside handlers as part of the reply step. The reply.view function accepts three parameters (the last one is optional): the relative path to the desired template file, the context to apply to the template, and an options object to override global and engine specific settings.

```
handler: function (request, reply) {

    var context = {
        content: 'hello world'
    };
    // assumes file can be found in views.path + '/path/
index'
    reply.view('path/index', context, { compileMode:
```

```
'sync' });
}
```

As a reminder, we do not need 'index.html' here, because we have already defined the extension in the `engines` portion of the `server.views` function.

Layouts

Layouts enable you to wrap all templates inside another one. This is useful if your website has the same general appearance (logo, header, and footer, for example). Then, you only need to design the HTML for a general layout and nest the normal template inside the `{{content}}` context variable.

Configuration

The most important step in enabling layouts is the configuration. Only two additional configuration fields are required: `layoutPath` and `layout`. The `layoutPath` tells hapi where to look to find `layout.{{ext}}`, where ext is the extension defined under the `engines` view option.

Configuration does not really change between the different templating systems.

```
var Hapi = require('hapi');

var server = new Hapi.Server();
server.views({
    engines: {
        html: require('handlebars') // .html is the suffix
hapi will look for
    },
    path: __dirname + '/views',
    layoutPath: __dirname + '/views',
    layout: true
});
```

Usage

Usage is actually very simple after a proper configuration. Nothing changes on the handler side:

```
handler: function (request, reply) {

    var ctx = {
        msg: 'Hello world!'
    };
    return reply.view('/path/' + 'templateName', ctx);
}
```

The template will be loaded through the **content** variable in the layout.

Exclusion

Sometimes you want to apply layouts to all templates, except for certain
ones. This is exceptionally easy to do. You just need to include a third optional configuration parameter to reply.view that sets layout to false.

```
// Inside an handler
return reply.view(template_name, context, { layout: false });
```

Partials

Partials are great. Partial templates allow you to factor out shared snippets of templates to use between other templates. This prevents you
from being forced to modify code in multiple places; you can edit once
and reflect in all templates.

Configuration

To enable partials, you need to add only a single view option, partialsPath, which tells hapi where to look for partials. Now when you reference partials, the paths will be relative to this path.

Configuration does not really change between the different templating systems. Some engines, however, may require small tweaks to work
with hapi's partial system. For example, for Hogan.js mustache templates, there is a convenient pre-tweaked version at **hapi-hogan**.

```
var Hapi = require('hapi');

var server = new Hapi.Server();
server.views({
    engines: {
```

```
        html: require('handlebars') // .html is the suffix
hapi will look for
    },
    path: __dirname + '/views',
    partialsPath: __dirname + '/views/partials'
});
```

Helpers

Helpers are extensions to the templating language that allow you to create and use custom functions from inside the template. This is a feature of Handlebars.js.

Configuration

To enable helpers, you need to supply only one additional view option `helpersPath`. This tells hapi where to find helpers files.

```
var Hapi = require('hapi');

var server = new Hapi.Server();
server.views({
    engines: {
        html: require('handlebars') // .html is the suffix
hapi will look for
    },
    path: __dirname + '/views',
    helpersPath: __dirname + '/views/helpers'
});
```

Helper Files

Helper files should be named with the desired calling name. If you want to create a helper function such as **toMoney**, the file should be called **toMoney.js** and it should module.export's a single function (which can take arguments).

```
module.exports = function (val) {

    return "$" + val.toFixed(2);
};
```

Then, inside the template, it will be possible to call **toMoney** with an argument (which could be variable).

```
{{toMoney 25}}
{{toMoney cost}}
```

Shared Contexts

It is often desirable to include some data into every context object of every view. For example, it is easier to maintain an HTML page title in one place and attach it to every view, rather than including it in every single view context.

The example below ('shared-context.js') will add (or overwrite) the **context.title** value with a new value. If the handler is not called with views, then, the **.context** will not be defined and it will not be affected.

```
server.ext('onPreResponse', function (request, reply) {

    var response = request.response;
    if (!response.isBoom) {
        if (response.source && response.source.context) {
            response.source.context.title = "Hapi-Plugins";
        }
    }

    return reply();
})
```

The above example is using **onPreResponse**, which we learned about in Chapter 2 Server, the request lifecycle chapter. We are using the **server.ext** to extend this functionality, so right before the response is given, we are adding this **title** context.

An alternative method is to merge a shared object into the view context:

```
// Inside the server.js
server.ext('onRequest', function (request, next) {

    // This could be loaded asynchronously from the database
    (and cached)
    request._sharedContext = {
        title: 'Hapi-Plugins'
    };
```

```
        next();
});
```

Here we are using the **onRequest** part of the request lifecycle instead. Like the previous example, we are extending this part of the request lifecycle by using the **server.ext** function. Below we use a handler to merge the **sharedContext** before we reply with the template.

```
// Inside the handler
var Hoek = require('hoek');
/* ... */
handler: function (request, reply) {

    var ctx = {
        content: 'Hello world!'
    };
    var context =
Hoek.applyToDefaults(request._sharedContext, ctx);
    return reply.view('/path/' + 'templateName', context);
}
```

By using a shared context, like above, it is possible to group common values shared between templates and views and place them in a single location (rather than repeating them in every handler and view). This is helpful if you need to repeatedly pass in server-wide settings like feature flags or website information or translations.

Summary

Now that you know how to render HTML to the end user given a data context, you can now create complete, functional websites using hapi. Views and templating systems can save you a lot of development time and make your life much easier by factoring out shared context data, shared partial templates, and entire templates.

Using the knowledge you have learned so far, you can now create fully functional websites using hapi. But, as you will see in Chapter 10 Testing, just being able to create a website is not enough. We will show you how to test your application.

Testing 10

In the last chapter (Chapter 9 Templating), we discovered how to respond to requests with HTML. With that final piece, you can create your own complete, fully functional web application. However, that is not enough! To build real, production-worthy applications, you will need to test your code.

In the hapi universe, testing is extremely important. Testing is important enough to the hapi module maintainers that they developed their own testing library, named lab, in order to get testing right. Before a pull request can be merged into a core module, it must first have working tests as well as 100% test coverage of the code in the module.

Therefore, if you plan to contribute back to the community, understanding how hapi tests are written and executed is essential.

Chapter Overview

The following chapter will cover many basic testing principles as well as the topics listed below:

- History of lab
- Installing lab
- Writing a simple test
- Principles of lab
- Writing a hapi test
- Code coverage
- Reporters
- Linting
- Plugin testing

History of lab

For best results, hapi works well with the lab test runner. Lab is the testing framework that was developed for use with hapi and hapi plugins. hapi originally used mocha and chai to execute tests. However, when Node.js 0.10 was released, hapi added support for the new release and incorporated domains. Domains have been a hairy feature ever since their release, testing support not excluded. When 0.10 was released, mocha was slow to adopt support for adequately testing domains. As a result of the desire for hapi to use domains, something had to be done. As a result, lab was created. Originally, lab was a fork of mocha. Features that were not needed for hapi were trimmed and more features were added.

Code coverage is an essential factor to ensuring that quality code is being committed to repositories. Therefore, code coverage support needs to be baked in to the testing framework as a simple flag when you run tests.

Before lab was created, mocha tests in hapi were being run with the blanket code coverage module. Blanket itself relies on esprima to create abstract syntax trees (AST) of the code in order to help identify statements to insert for code coverage analysis. Blanket was carried over into lab when lab was created. However, over time, code coverage support was baked into lab, instead of being delivered through a third party.

Code coverage reporting also evolved as a result of incorporating the analysis within lab. This helps to make code coverage a first class citizen in lab reports. As a result, the HTML reporter now indicates to the developer the lines in their code that will never be reachable by tests.
This makes it easy to identify areas of code that are dead and can be deleted, making your code even more maintainable as a result.

When hapi was using mocha for testing, it was also using chai to help structure the assertions. The hapi maintainers favor writing tests using the expect style, as opposed to should or assert. Over time, however, the use of chai surfaced a couple of edge case function names that weren't consistent with the larger framework. For example, the exist property isn't executed as a function, unlike some of the other parts of the syntax. These inconsistencies led to a few bugs popping up from time to time. These bugs had to do with the fact that it was too easy to forget a method () and it would result in an assertion that was never executed. Because it was never executed, it therefore passed incorrectly.

As a result, the testing assertion library named code was created. Code takes the chai syntax and makes exist become a function, just as all of the 'truthy' checks for true, false, and null become functions. Below you can see the differences between chai and code.

First our chai example is:

```
expect(foo).to.exist;
expect(bar).to.be.true;
```

Next you can see our code example for doing the same thing. Notice that true and exist are functions in code.

```
expect(foo).to.exist();
expect(bar).to.be.true();
```

In addition to the inconsistencies described earlier, we wanted an assertion library that was small, simple, and intuitive. Logic was stripped out that was dealing with plugins, extensions, and the overhead of supporting testing the browser. This resulted in much of the same functionality that we needed, but it resulted in about 300 lines that is trivial to read and understand.

Finally, code allowed deeper integration between the test runner and the assertion library. This allowed us to get total assertion counts to measure the tests' comprehensiveness and to verify that every assertion created is indeed executed.

Lab has evolved in other ways as well. For example, transpiler support has been added to support testing CoffeeScript or JSX code. Additionally, lab now has linting support baked in, so that pull requests to hapi repositories follow the same coding style. This has been useful for developers to know ahead of time if they are violating any style guide rules ahead of asking for a commit to be merged. One of the current drawbacks to lab, however, is that it's designed and runs only on the server at this point. However, this will likely change as its popularity grows and more developers desire to use it for client-side testing.

Installing lab

Lab may be useful to install globally in your environment. Similarly to other node.js modules, the installation of lab can be accomplished by using npm. This is shown below.

```
$ npm install -g lab
```

While you can install lab globally, in general you don't need to. Instead, all of the hapi core modules include lab in the devDependencies section of the package.json. Any recent version of lab is fine to install globally and locally, as the two won't conflict when running tests. The next example shows how to install lab only locally and save it to the devDependencies section of the package.json.

```
$ npm install lab --save-dev
```

After you have installed lab you should verify that it's working correctly. If installed globally, lab will be available in the PATH environment variable. Otherwise, you will need to run the lab binary from the node_modules/.bin folder. To verify a global lab install, simply run lab -h. If you want to verify a local install, then you need to run node ./node_modules/.bin/lab -h. You should get the help page for lab.

As an aside, it may be helpful to auto-update your PATH when navigating into a folder with children node_modules/.bin folders. This will make local binaries runnable the same way as global binaries are.

Installing code

Similar to how lab was installed, you should also install code. Remember, lab doesn't have a built-in assert library that is included out-of-the-box. Therefore, you should use code, chai, or any of the other assert modules that you prefer. You can, again, run npm install code --save-dev to save this in your package.json file or add it in manually.

Writing a simple test

All tests should be located in a test folder within the root of your project. This is a pattern that is nearly ubiquitous in the Node.js community. How you choose to name your test files is up to you, as there isn't an established naming convention across the board. However, a pattern that is used throughout the modules in the *hapi* organization is to name each test file the same as the corresponding module that it's responsible for testing. For the purposes of this exercise, create a file in `test` named `index.js`. Populate `index.js` with the code found below.

```
// Load modules

var Code = require('code');
var Lab = require('lab');


var lab = exports.lab = Lab.script();

lab.test('lab exists', function (done) {

    Code.expect(lab).to.exist();
    done();
});
```

Simply type the command `lab` in the root of the project to run the test above. The output will look like following:

```
$ lab

  .

1 tests complete
Test duration: 5 ms
No global variable leaks detected
```

Hopefully that wasn't difficult or shocking. As you can see from the output, the time it takes to run the test is reported along with a default reporter for dot notations.

Principles of lab

Let's take a look at the core lab principles to keep in mind.

Always asynchronous

In the previous section, you saw what a simple `lab` test looks like. One of the defining characteristics of `lab` is that tests are always assumed to be asynchronous. Instead of inspecting the `length` of the `arguments` object and running tests differently that have an argument for `done`, all `lab` tests must receive a callback argument and execute it when the test is complete. If an argument wasn't expected by the test, then the test immediately fails with an explanation. Take for example, the test below:

```
// Load modules

var Code = require('code');
var Lab = require('lab');


var lab = exports.lab = Lab.script();

lab.test('lab exists', function () {

    Code.expect(lab).to.exist();
});
```

When we run lab we get the following output:

```
$ lab

Error: Function for test "lab exists" should take exactly
one argument
```

Similarly, if an argument is accepted in the test function but isn't executed, an error will occur. However, this time the error will be a timeout for the test itself. We can have it timeout by removing **done()**. This can be done by writing the following test.

```
// Load modules

var Code = require('code');
var Lab = require('lab');


var lab = exports.lab = Lab.script();

lab.test('lab exists', function (done) {

    Code.expect(lab).to.exist();
});
```

The resulting output for this test will look as follows:

```
$ lab

    x
```

```
Failed tests:

  1)  lab exists:

      Timed out (2000ms) -  lab exists


1 of 1 tests failed
Test duration: 2007 ms
No global variable leaks detected
```

Notice, in the previous example that the . is changed to an x to indicate a failed test. If you want to make the reporting more explicit, you can enable verbose mode with -v. Below is an example of verbose mode enabled with the same test.

```
$ lab -v
☐1) lab exists


Failed tests:

  1)  lab exists:

      Timed out (2000ms) -  lab exists


1 of 1 tests failed
Test duration: 2006 ms
No global variable leaks detected
```

Test scripts

Lab also doesn't assume that a JavaScript file in the test folder is necessarily a test. Therefore, in order to tell lab that a script file is a test script, you must execute Lab.script() and assign the result to the lab property of the module.exports object. In order to help catch developer mistakes with this style, lab will report any instances when script() was executed but a lab property wasn't exported. An example of this code is shown here:

```
// Load modules

var Code = require('code');
```

```
var Lab = require('lab');


var lab = Lab.script();

lab.test('lab exists', function (done) {

    Code.expect(lab).to.exist();
    done();
});
```

With this test, if you run lab, the error message for this mistake would look like:

```
$ lab
The file: test/index.js includes a lab script that is not
exported via exports.lab
```

Safe globals

Another assumption of lab is that the global object shouldn't be polluted with test features. Whereas other frameworks will attach a describe or it to the global object, lab tries a different approach of trying to isolate each experiment. Each of the experiment or test functions is only available on a lab object that's returned by executing script().

Lab takes the global issue a step further and checks the global object for any new properties that exist after running tests. This is usually a sign of a missing var when declaring a variable. However, this feature can be disabled by passing -l or --leaks to the lab binary. Similarly, if there is a known global that should exist you can pass it as an argument to -I or --ignore. For example, if you want to ignore a property named foo, set on the global object, you would execute lab as follows:

```
$ lab --ignore foo
```

Experiments

While lab tests can be made to look like mocha and jasmine behavior driven development (BDD) style tests, they can also be be named something else entirely. Whereas BDD styles tend to use describe and it, lab also offers the options to use experiment and test instead. The functions describe and experiment are interchangeable, just as it and **test** are. The style you choose is entirely up to you, and there isn't a wrong answer. One of the things that is nice about using the **experi-ments** style, however, is that it does reinforce the notion that an engineer is creating the tests and that there is some attempt to be scientific about them.

An experiment is useful for wrapping a group of similar tests. For example, if you are testing **lab** itself, you may write experiment tests that are wrapped in an experiment as demonstrated below.

```
// Load modules

var Code = require('code');
var Lab = require('lab');


var lab = exports.lab = Lab.script();

lab.experiment('lab', function () {

    lab.test('exists', function (done) {

        Code.expect(lab).to.exist();
        done();
    });

    lab.test('has properties', function (done) {

        Code.expect(Object.keys(lab)).to.not.have.length(0);
        done();
    });
});
```

Then if you run these tests in verbose mode, you will get the following:

```
$ $ lab -v
  lab
    ☐ 1) exists (3 ms)
    ☐ 2) has properties (1 ms)


  2 tests complete
  Test duration: 6 ms
  No global variable leaks detected
```

You can see here that with verbose mode, you can also see how long each test took.

Writing a hapi test

hapi was designed with testing in mind. In order to ship a release, every line and every code path must have a test written for it. As a result, there are quite a lot of tests in hapi and its dependencies. In order to help speed up the time it takes to run tests, as well as avoid issues with file descriptor limits, hapi has built-in mock request support. This is delivered through a function named inject provided by the module *shot*. To help illustrate the power of shot look at the test below. Also notice that instead of using the experiment style of testing, the test is written with test shortcuts for the BDD style.

```
// Load modules

var Code = require('code');
var Hapi = require('hapi');
var Lab = require('lab');


var lab = exports.lab = Lab.script();
var describe = lab.describe;
var it = lab.it;
var expect = Code.expect;


describe('inject()', function () {

    it('returns the response result', function (done) {

        var handler = function (request, reply) {

            return reply('hello');
        };

        var server = new Hapi.Server();
        server.connection();
        server.route({
            method: 'GET',
            path: '/',
            config: { handler: handler }
        });
```

```
        server.inject('/', function (res) {

            expect(res.statusCode).to.equal(200);
            expect(res.result).to.equal('hello');
            done();
        });
    });
});
```

In the previous example the **server.start** function wasn't executed. As a result, no socket was created or attached to by the server. However, a request was made to the server and a response was received. The request object includes all of the properties that a hapi server cares about. Similarly, the response object passed to the **inject** callback includes the response body and relevant headers and status code information.

Unless the test you are creating needs information from a socket, the best solution is usually to use **inject**. If this is the approach you take then your tests should execute much faster than if they relied on a real socket. Also, it makes it much easier to avoid the setup and teardown associated with a socket. Speaking of which, if you need to use a socket, pass 0 as the **port** to the **connection** function in order to ensure that the port is available. The code below illustrates this. Notice that the port that ends up being used can be retrieved from the **server.info.port** property after a server is started.

```
// Load modules

var Code = require('code');
var Hapi = require('hapi');
var Lab = require('lab');
var Wreck = require('wreck');


var lab = exports.lab = Lab.script();
var describe = lab.describe;
var it = lab.it;
var expect = Code.expect;


describe('real request', function () {

    it('returns a real response', function (done) {

        var handler = function (request, reply) {
```

```
            return reply('hello');
        };

        var server = new Hapi.Server();
        server.connection({ port: 0 });
        server.route({
            method: 'GET',
            path: '/',
            config: { handler: handler } });

        server.start(function () {

            Wreck.get('http://localhost:' +
                    server.info.port,
                function (err, res, payload) {

                    expect(res.statusCode).to.equal(200);
                    expect(payload).to.equal('hello');
                    server.stop(done);
                });
            });
        });
    });
});
```

Wreck is a lightweight HTTP/HTTPS client request wrapper that was designed for hapi. This is the module of choice when doing any requests. That being said, the `request` module is completely supported as well. Locally, the difference in test time between the `inject` example and the `wreck` example is around 18ms.

Even though 18ms on its own isn't a lot, all of the tests you create can quickly add up.

Code coverage

Aside from all of the previous features that go into `lab`, code coverage is one its strongest features. Code coverage in *lab* depends on the *espree* module for generating the AST. Other than typical line by line coverage, *lab* will also determine if different code branches are executed by tests. This can be anything from many conditionals within the same `if` statement to standard ternary statements. Furthermore, *lab* will also determine if a code path is unable to be executed, and can therefore be deleted.

The 'html' and 'console' reporters are the most heavily tested when it comes to showing code coverage. By default, code coverage isn't enabled when you run lab. To enable it you need to pass in the -c or --coverage flags. The coverage flag will enable code coverage reporting and expect that the tests cover 100% of the code. If you expect less than 100% code coverage then you can use the -t or --threshold flag following by a number that represents the percent of code covered before throwing an error. If the tests fail to pass the threshold, lab exits with an error code.

Below there is an output of the console reporter that shows what failed test coverage looks like.

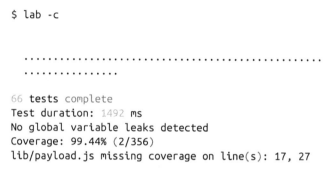

```
$ lab -c


  ..................................................
  ..................

66 tests complete
Test duration: 1492 ms
No global variable leaks detected
Coverage: 99.44% (2/356)
lib/payload.js missing coverage on line(s): 17, 27
```

If this isn't detailed enough and you need a better overview of missing coverage, then using the 'html' reporter is recommended. To use a different reporter, simply pass the name of the reporter to the -r or --reporter flag. You can see below a screenshot of the output from running lab -c -r html > coverage.html.

```
12
13      module.exports = internals.Payload = function (payload, encoding) {
14
15          Stream.Readable.call(this);
16
17          var data = [].concat(payload || '');
18          var size = 0;
19          for (var i = 0, il = data.length; i < il; ++i) {
20              var chunk = data[i];
21              size += chunk.length;
22              data[i] = Buffer.isBuffer(chunk) ? chunk : new Buffer(chunk);
23          }
24
25          this._data = Buffer.concat(data, size);
26          this._position = 0;
27          this._encoding = encoding || 'utf8';
28      };
29
```

As you can see, coverage is missing on line 17 and 27 only in very specific variables. However, if you add tests for the missing variables on those lines, you can see the result of running the 'console' reporter in next example.

```
$ lab -c
```

```
....................................................
....................
```

```
69 tests complete
Test duration: 1494 ms
No global variable leaks detected
Coverage: 100.00%
```

Using coverage is a must when it comes to developing modules in the hapi ecosystem. All of the modules published under the hapijs organization demand 100% code coverage. Therefore, if you plan to contribute any changes or enhancements to these modules you must add tests for the changed code. There may be naysayers when it comes to code coverage, but it's the mechanism that has been chosen to help gauge if code works. In addition to adding tests that cover every line and code path in a module, hapijs maintainers also review the tests and code to help ensure its accuracy. A person can cover a line with a test that checks a wrong assumption, engineers are ultimately responsible for checking the code and the tests.

Reporters

Lab comes packed with numerous reporters as well as support for any custom reporters. The reporters have evolved over the years from feedback from the community. Currently, lab supporters the following reporters.

- console - CLI output
- html - report to an html stream, pipe to a file
- json - JSON formatted report
- junit - JUnit XML format
- tap - TAP format
- lcov - lcov format
- clover - clover XML format
- custom

Previously, in the code coverage section, the 'console' and 'html' reporters were demonstrated as it relates to reporting coverage. However, the 'html' reporter does more, it also reports on the tests run and how long each took. An example of the 'html' reporter as it relates to individual tests is shown here:

Test Report

0 Failures 0 Skipped 66 Tests (1450 ms)

☑ Show Success ☐ Show Failure ☑ request() ☑ read() ☑ parseCacheControl() ☑ Shortcut ☑ json ☑ Events

ID	Title	Duration (ms)
1	request() requests a resource with callback	21
2	request() requests a POST resource	6
3	request() requests a POST resource with unicode characters in payload	5
4	request() requests a POST resource with headers	3
5	request() requests a POST resource with stream payload	5
6	request() requests a resource without callback	2
7	request() cannot set agent and rejectUnauthorized at the same time	1
8	request() cannot set a false agent and rejectUnauthorized at the same time	0
9	request() can set a null agent and rejectUnauthorized at the same time	12
10	request() requests an https resource	345
11	request() requests an https resource with secure protocol set	297
12	request() fails when an https resource has invalid certs and the default rejectUnauthorized	11
13	request() succeeds when an https resource has unauthorized certs and rejectUnauthorized is false	7
14	request() requests a resource with downstream dependency	6
15	request() does not follow redirections by default	3
16	request() handles redirections	4
17	request() handles redirections with relative location	5
18	request() reaches max redirections count	3

If you plan to use `lab` with Jenkins then the `junit` reporter may be a good choice because many Jenkins plugins rely on this format like dashboard-view. You could also use the HTML reporter in combination with the HTML publisher plugin for a detailed view of the tests and code coverage. The `json` reporter is a nice native reporter you can easily parse if you need to look at the raw data to do your own parsing. It reports on code coverage as well as general test failures. Shown below is an example of the output from the `json` reporter with code coverage enabled using the `-c` flag.

```
"17": {
    "source": "      var data = [].concat(payload || '');",
    "chunks": [
      {
        "source": "      var data = [].concat("
      },
      {
        "source": "payload",
        "miss": "true"
      },
      {
        "source": " || "
      },
      {
        "source": "''",
        "miss": "never"
      },
      {
        "source": ");"
      }
    ],
    "hits": 4,
    "miss": true
}
```

As you can see above, the miss is reported on the line and individual code branch, if there happens to be one. This allows the tool reading the JSON output to more easily parse and represent the missed code. Additionally, you can see the number of executions that hit this line, but ended up missing the code branch.

Each line number is represented as the key name in the parent object. Each JSON entry starts with the code file information that coverage is checked against, which can be viewed here:

```json
{
    "filename": "lib/payload.js",
    "percent": 92.5925925925926,
    "hits": 25,
    "misses": 2,
    "sloc": 27,
    "source": {
        "1": {
        "source": "",
        "miss": false
    }
}
```

Additionally, the JSON reporter, like the 'html' reporter, includes information about individual tests executed. Every test name is displayed along with execution duration and, most importantly, if the test passed or not. This part of the JSON output is shown below.

```json
{
    "tests": {
        "request()": [
            {
                "title": "requests a resource with callback",
                "err": false,
                "duration": 23
            },
            {
                "title": "requests a POST resource",
                "err": false,
                "duration": 5
            }
        ]
    }
}
```

Linting

One of the powerful features that lab includes is built-in linting support. Out of the box, eslint and jshint are supported linters. The default linting rules enforce a style like the hapi style guide. The original intent of including the linters is to ensure that pull requests to hapi projects follow the same style. However, the linting rules can be changed to fit the needs of your project. Any options that need to be passed into the linter can be set using the --lint-options argument. If you want to run the default linting rules with the default linter, eslint, then you pass -L or --lint to `lab`. In order to change the linter used, pass `-n` or `--linter` to `lab`. Below demonstrates how to run `lab` with jshint.

```
$ lab -n jshint
```

Plugin Testing

As you build plugins and servers using hapi, one of the things that you will need to do is test that a plugin can be registered and that a server can be started. For the hapi-plugins.com site we used `lab` to write the tests.

One of the common tests, which exists throughout plugins in the hapi ecosystem, is that of checking that a plugin can be registered with hapi itself. Below tests if the hapi-plugins.com plugin can be registered within hapi and if the server can be started:

```javascript
// Load modules

var Code = require('code');
var Lab = require('lab');
var HapiPlugins = require('../');


// Test shortcuts

var lab = exports.lab = Lab.script();
var describe = lab.describe;
var it = lab.it;
var expect = Code.expect;

describe('hapi plugins', function () {

    it('Server can be started', function (done) {

        HapiPlugins.init(function (err, server) {

            expect(err).to.not.exist();
            expect(server).to.exist();
            done();
        });
    });
});
```

With hapi-plugins.com we are using a database. Therefore, we are in need of validating that the database actually works. As we try to test everything, integration testing as well as testing with mocks are both useful. A common test may be to test that you can create a connection to a database and save data to the database. Below demonstrates a complete test that performs work to and from a database. Notice that the tests use the `inject` function to call the server route in order to retrieve the plugin that was just saved. This example is an excellent reference of a pattern you can reuse in your code.

```
// Load modules

var Code = require('code');
var Lab = require('lab');
var HapiPlugins = require('../');


// Test shortcuts

var lab = exports.lab = Lab.script();
var describe = lab.describe;
var it = lab.it;
var expect = Code.expect;

describe('hapi plugins', function () {

    it('can like a plugin', function (done) {

        var resetDb = function (callback) {

            DB.plugin.remove(function (err) {

                if (err) {
                    return callback(err);
                }

                DB.user.remove(callback);
            });
        };

        resetDb(function (err) {

            expect(err).to.not.exist();

            HapiPlugins.init(function (err, server) {

                expect(err).to.not.exist();

                var plugin = DB.plugin({
```

```
                    name: 'purdy',
                    license: 'MIT',
                    version: '1.0.1',
                    description: 'a niceties plugin',
                    authors: ['daniel']
                });

                var options = {
                    url: '/plugins/purdy/like',
                    method: 'GET'
                };

                plugin.save(function (err) {

                    expect(err).to.not.exist();

                    server.inject(options, function
(response) {

expect(response.result.success).to.equal(true);
                        done();
                    });
                });
            });
        });
    });
});
```

Summary

In this chapter, we covered how testing is central to the hapi ecosystem. Without testing and the tooling built around the hapi testing framework, *lab*, it would be far more difficult to ensure that quality code is delivered. When you contribute back to any of the core hapi modules you will need to be familiar with how to create tests and cover any new code 100% of the way with tests. Additionally, when writing code for any of the hapi core modules, use *lab* to help ensure that the hapi style guide is being followed.

The tests and tooling around them in hapi can always be improved. If you are looking for a good starting point to jump into contributing back to the hapi ecosystem, please take a look at writing tests for modules. Even though the various modules have 100% code coverage, further testing can be useful in many cases.

In the next chapter, we will show you some powerful methods used to debug your hapi systems and identify major issues.

Debugging 11

A debugged program is one for which you have not yet found the conditions that make it fail.

-- Jerry Ogdin

In the last chapter, we learned a lot about how to test hapi applications and how to write unit tests. In this chapter, we'll discover how to debug our hapi applications using some advanced tools.

Debugging in Node.js has always been a source of pain for many developers. There is still a lack of great tooling to help developers with debugging Node.js across platforms and throughout an applications full lifecycle. While tools like DTrace exist, not all Node.js deployments have the opportunity to use it. Joyent and other companies have done a great job at documenting how to debug a Node.js application. In the hapi world, we have created modules to help make debugging a hapi application even easier. This chapter will cover specific hapi modules that can help with debugging a hapi server in different environments. Additionally, this chapter covers how to setup reporting that can help diagnose issues.

Chapter Overview

The following chapter will cover many details on debugging hapi and Node.js in general. These topics are:

- console.log
- debug mode
- TV
- Good
- REPL

- Heap Snapshots
- Core Files

console.log

While many developers may look down on console.log as a viable de-bugging option, it serves a purpose and can be quite useful. There are many instances where you simply need to know the value of a variable at a certain point in a remote deployment. For situations like this, where a REPL or a remote debugging session can be overkill, don't look down on using console.log. When it comes to the scripting nature of node.js and how quickly a process can be started it is simple to *ssh* into a server and add a log statement. While not the most elegant, it can help identify state at different points in your application.

debug mode

Fortunately, in hapi there is also the concept of a debug mode. Instead of manually going in and typing a bunch of console.log statements within hapi, you can start a server in debug mode and have console access to different server events and error details. As this mode can be verbose and is not necessary for production, it is recommended that you only enable debug mode for development. Below is an example of starting a server in debug mode and logging all errors to the console.

```
var Hapi = require('hapi');

var options = {
    debug: {
        log: ['error']
    }
};

var server = new Hapi.Server(options);
server.connection({ port: 8000 });

server.route({ method: 'GET', path: '/', handler: function
(request, reply) {

    throw new Error('Tribbles');
}});
```

```
server.start(function () {

    console.log('server started');
});

Debug: internal, implementation, error
    Error: Uncaught error: Tribbles
```

As you can see in the previous example, when an error occurs, the error and the stack trace is logged to the console with **Debug:** prefixing the log statement.

TV

Another useful option for debugging hapi servers, in development, is with the use of the *tv* module. TV was designed primarily for front-end and consumers of a hapi application. The goal is to provide an easy to use dashboard that displays information about server request activity. This is especially useful for a front-end developer to be able to track the lifecycle of a request that their code makes to a hapi server. A screenshot of *tv* is shown here:

In order to add *tv* to a server, you register it like any other hapi plugin. Below shows how to register **tv** with the default settings. After **tv** is registered on a server you can access it at your server URL + **/debug/console**.

```
var Hapi = require('hapi');
var Tv = require('tv');

var server = new Hapi.Server();
```

```
server.connection();

server.register(Tv, function (err) {

    if (!err) {
        server.start(function(){
          console.log('server started');
        });
    }
});
```

With *tv* you can subscribe to request events that you care about by selecting the different tags for the events. The request details are sent in real-time to the *tv* page as they are made. If any requests stand out as something that is useful you can also star and investigate them.

Good

Logging request details in *tv* is useful for local development. However, when you are in QA or production you will want to use a module designed specifically for that scenario. For these situations, as well as for local development, the *good* plugin is extremely useful.

What makes *good* even more appropriate for QA and production is that it is designed to also log operations data. Over the years this has been expanded to not only include the typical memory or CPU details, but also it now includes event loop delay and network activity.

To add *good* to a hapi server you register it like any other plugin. The major difference is that with *good* you will need to specify options for the types of events you care about and where to log those events. *good* events include the following:

- ops
- response
- log
- error
- request
- wreck

Where event data can be stored is quite extensive. If you need a different reporter, you can build one by looking at one of the many examples. The available reporters for *good* currently includes the following types:

- UDP

- HTTP
- Files
- Console
- InfluxDB
- Winston
- Loggly
- Logstash

This list will continue to grow. You get get the latest list by looking at the **good** page. The code below shows how to register *good* and log all ops data to a file under /var/log/example/ops.json every second.

```
var Hapi = require('hapi');
var Good = require('good');

var server = new Hapi.Server();
server.connection();

var options = {
    opsInterval: 1000,
    reporters: [{
        reporter: 'good-file',
        events: { ops: '*' },
        config: '/var/log/example/ops.json'
    }]
};

server.register({
    register: Good,
    options: options
}, function (err) {

    if (err) {
        console.error(err);
        return;
    }

    server.start(function(){
      console.log('server started');
    });
});
```

When you look at the ops log file you will notice that each of the entries is JSON.parse-able and each entry is delimited by a newline. Below is a sample of what the event data looks like.

```json
{
    "event": "ops",
    "timestamp": 1527940993174,
    "host": "mac.local",
    "pid": 35503,
    "os": {
        "load": [2.13427734375,2.44287109375,
            2.4873046875],
        "mem": {
            "total": 17179869184,
            "free": 5757075456},
        "uptime":459461
    },
    "proc": {
        "uptime": 4,
        "mem":{
            "rss": 46538752,
            "heapTotal": 32171264,
            "heapUsed": 17638880
        },
        "delay": 0.2207310050725937},
        "load": {
            "requests": {},
            "concurrents": {"62778": 0},
            "responseTimes": {},
            "sockets": {
                "http": {
                    "total":0
                },
                "https": {
                    "total":0
                }
            }
        }
    }
}
```

In the previous example, you can see that there is a lot of useful information that is logged. It makes it possible to correlate higher than usual memory use with network activity or the event loop being slow.

In *good* version 6 and later there is support for logging request data made with *wreck*. This is useful for tracking down issues that may exist between your hapi server and downstream servers. The hapi reverse proxy module depends on *wreck*, therefore, the reverse proxy data can be logged using *good*.

An example of output when you use *wreck* support may look like the following:

```
{"event":"wreck","timestamp":1431469615889,"timeSpent":
581,"request":{"method":"GET","path":"/api/
route","url":"http://localhost:8081/api/
route","protocol":"http:","host":"localhost","headers":
{"host":"localhost:8081"}},"response":{"statusCode":
200,"statusMessage":"OK","headers":{"content-
type":"application/json; charset=utf-8","cache-control":"no-
cache","content-length":"4198","accept-
ranges":"bytes","date":"Tue, 12 May 2015 22:26:55
GMT","connection":"close"}}}
```

You can see there is some great information here. You can, for example, graph `timeSpent` and find out in your calls how much of your time is spent using the dependent service. It can also be very useful to look at your headers to make sure they are getting sent properly.

There is a great deal of power available from the data that *good* collects and reports. Business, as well as operations people, should find the information useful. Sending the data to a log aggregrator like Splunk or logstash and then creating dashboards for the different stakeholders in your application is a good way to leverage the data available. This can be a powerful and easy win for your hapi application.

In the case of the hapi-plugins.com project, *good* is used to log operations and *hapi* log events to the console. This was accomplished in the `index.js` file inside of the `lib` folder by registering *good* along with the *good-console* reporter. An example of this registration is found below.

```
var goodOptions = {
    opsInterval: 5000,
    reporters: [{
        reporter: 'good-console',
        events: { log: '*', ops: '*' }
    }]
};

var registerHttpPlugins = function (next) {
    server.register([
        Bell,
        Blipp,
        HapiAuthCookie,
        Authentication,
        Controllers,
        Models,
        Routes,
        { register: require('good'), options: goodOptions }
    ],
    { select: 'http' },
```

```
function (err) {

    return next(err);
});
};
```

The events that the *good-console* reporter will send to the console are indicated by the **events** property. The * value indicates that the reporter will not filter out any events based on specific tags. If you are concerned with only events related to a certain tag, then you can indicate so by replacing * with a single string named the same as the tag you care about or with an array of strings representing the event tags you care about.

The reporting from *good* is observed after you start the server and look at the output to **stdio**. Below shows an example output from the **ops** event after 10 seconds of the server running. As you can see, the memory consumed, uptime, and the load values can be reported on.

```
150418/175554.526, [ops], memory: 64Mb, uptime (seconds): 5,
load: 1.646484375,2.1015625,1.76806640625
150418/175559.531, [ops], memory: 65Mb, uptime (seconds):
10, load: 1.67431640625,2.099609375,1.76904296875
```

REPL

In order to make it easier to debug running applications on remote servers the *hapi* plugin *reptile* was created.

This plugin creates a REPL that listens on a port for TCP connections that have access to the running *hapi* server object. A REPL is a read execute print loop, and is a great way to modify a running server or simply inspect what is happening on it. By default, the REPL is only accessible from the **localhost**. This is done by design, in order to prevent anyone from gaining access to the REPL, which has the potential to cause issues on the application.

The REPL that is accessible on the port is the same one that you get when you type **node** without any arguments. Both are using the **repl** module that ships with node core. The only difference is that **server** is added to the global context.

In order to create a connection to the REPL port, you can use netcat or telnet. When you run the server in the **/example** folder inside of *reptile*, it will create a dummy server and register the *reptile* plugin. The example server listens on port 9000. Below is how you connect using net-cat to the local port 9000.

```
$ nc localhost 9000
>
```

After a connection is established you should see what objects are available on the global object. To do this, simply type `global` and press Enter. From this point, you can navigate through existing objects or create handlers for events. This should provide a nice hook into the running server that you can use for debugging purposes.

Heap Snapshots

Some of the most difficult problems to debug are those that cause your process to crash. A common method for debugging these issues is to simply look at the stack output when the exception occurs. Another useful tool in the world of v8 is to create a snapshot of the heap at the moment the exception takes place and analyze it later. To help address both of these use cases the module *poop* was created. The module *poop* is a hapi plugin that listens for the process `uncaughtException` event to fire. When an uncaught exception occurs, a heap snapshot file is created and the exception details are logged to a file. *Poop* will also rethrow the exception so that the exception can propagate and be handled by other event subscribers.

The heap snapshot files end with the extension `.heapsnapshot`. These files can be opened with the chrome v8 web inspector. To open a file, launch the web inspector and select the "Profiles" tab, then click the "Load" button to open a snapshot file. The screenshot here shows what this tab looks like in the inspector.

After you select the heap snapshot in the profile tab, you can drill into the objects on the heap. Not only that, but the profile tab also lists the size of each of the objects on the heap. This is useful for helping to identify memory leaks in an application, as you can often find large numbers of objects consuming a large percentage of the servers' memory. A screenshot of the selected heap snapshot in the profile tab is shown here.

Core Files

One of the more powerful tools to use when debugging an issue with a Node process is to drop a core file of the running process and investigate it with the modular debugging (mdb) tool in SmartOS. Core files are now able to be created on Linux and analyzed in SmartOS. To create a core on Linux you will need to have a newer version of node and the ulimit set to unlimited. Many of the process analysis tools like pmap and pfiles are SmartOS only. This may be enough of a reason for people to stay with strictly SmartOS versus dumping on Linux only to have to analyze it on SmartOS later. But the option for Linux cores does exist.

Joyent has made an effort to improve the support for debugging node.js on SmartOS by adding commands to mdb that can be loaded aftera Node core is loaded. In Node 0.12.0 and later there are now commands, also known as dcmds, which include nodebuffer, jsfunctions, jssource, and v8internal. This is on top of the already great list of dcmds available, such as findjsobjects, jsstack, and jsprint among others.

You can use mdb by either attaching to a running process or by passing in a core file as the argument. Generally, you will find that you are looking at an existing core file. If you are attaching to a running process you need to pass the process pid to the p argument to mdb. After you are attached or a core is loaded you should load the v8 support into mdb by typing ::load v8. If you need to load from a specific v8.so you can point to the full file path. Here is what this process looks like in bash:

```
# mdb corefile
Loading modules: [ libumem.so.1 libc.so.1 ld.so.1 ]
> ::load v8
V8 version: 3.14.5.9
Autoconfigured V8 support from target
C++ symbol demangling enabled
```

Generally, the next step is to investigate the stack at the time the core was taken. To do this you use the dcmd jsstack to print the stack. To get extra information for the stack you should pass in the -v argument for verbose mode. This will print the stack trace with related memory addresses for the stack. These items in memory can be inspected further by passing the address into the ::jsprint dcmd. The next example demonstrates taking a jsstack and passing it into jsprint and displaying the result.

```
> ::jsstack -v
...
d7fffdf8bc0 0x4a14afaca2c8 <anonymous> (as Agent.addRequest)
(6e1f064b3aa1)
    file: http.js
    arg1: 67d9962cf1d1 (JSObject)
    arg2: 67d9962c2041 (SeqAsciiString)
    arg3: 3bb00000000 (SMI: value = 443)
    arg4: 60bc59304121 (Oddball: "undefined")
...
> 6e1f064b3aa1::jsprint
function <anonymous> (as Agent.addRequest)
```

Another useful dcmd is findjsobjects, which will print all of the JavaScript objects that can be found in the core file. Using this command you can sometimes find memory leaks simply because it prints out the number of objects that exist in memory that match the related signature. You can pipe the results from findjsobjects into jsprint to display the contents of each of the objects.

Outside of mdb are several useful process tools that will work on a core file created in SmartOS. These are usually found in /usr/proc/bin and include the following commands:

```
# pwd
/usr/proc/bin
# ls -l
total 13
lrwxrwxrwx 1 root root 15 Jun 29 2013 pcred -> ../../bin/
pcred
lrwxrwxrwx 1 root root 16 Jun 29 2013 pfiles -> ../../bin/
pfiles
lrwxrwxrwx 1 root root 16 Jun 29 2013 pflags -> ../../bin/
pflags
lrwxrwxrwx 1 root root 14 Jun 29 2013 pldd -> ../../bin/pldd
lrwxrwxrwx 1 root root 14 Jun 29 2013 pmap -> ../../bin/pmap
lrwxrwxrwx 1 root root 14 Jun 29 2013 prun -> ../../bin/prun
lrwxrwxrwx 1 root root 14 Jun 29 2013 psig -> ../../bin/psig
lrwxrwxrwx 1 root root 16 Jun 29 2013 pstack -> ../../bin/
pstack
lrwxrwxrwx 1 root root 15 Jun 29 2013 pstop -> ../../bin/
pstop
lrwxrwxrwx 1 root root 15 Jun 29 2013 ptime -> ../../bin/
ptime
lrwxrwxrwx 1 root root 15 Jun 29 2013 ptree -> ../../bin/
ptree
lrwxrwxrwx 1 root root 15 Jun 29 2013 pwait -> ../../bin/
pwait
lrwxrwxrwx 1 root root 14 Jun 29 2013 pwdx -> ../../bin/pwdx
```

Of the above process tools, the pmap and pfiles are especially useful. pmap displays the memory map of the core file, including how much memory is occupied by the heap and buffer areas. pfiles is able to report on file descriptors used by the process that created the core file. This can be useful for identifying when a ulimit isn't high enough. Sometimes, using pfiles can also help find situations where files aren't being closed correctly and are left open. pflags is able to report on the original command that started the process.

Summary

In this chapter we looked at different tooling that exists to debug hapi processes. These include specialty tools that were generated for the sole purpose of helping to identify issues in hapi servers. Using *good* for logging or *tv* for local debugging can be helpful. For production issues, using core files or a REPL can also be useful. For any issue that you find that exists in hapi itself, be sure to file an issue in the hapi github repo.

Security 12

In Chapter 11, we learned about the various ways to debug our apps. Now that our application behaves as expected, we need to ensure it continues to behave despite any malicious actions from hackers.

Security is a vital part of web development. But since it may often be complex or scary for new developers, it is not often included in typical beginner tutorials or documentation. As such, new web applications do not normally include any protection and become ripe targets for hackers (malicious or otherwise).

Large websites are not immune by default. One of the more famous (yet more prankish than devastating) **exploits** affected Facebook. In fact, there are some **companies** whose employees may or may not have accidentally harmed a competitor's product through XSS.

By covering your bases early, you can prevent the most common attack vectors and give yourself peace of mind.

This chapter exposes some of the more common problems and vulnerabilities, as well as their solutions.

Best practices

Follow along to learn about best security practices to implement when using hapi.

Password hashing: BCrypt

When storing user login passwords in the database, it is very bad practice to store passwords in plain text. Should a malicious hacker gain access to the database, they can directly use those credentials immediately to cause great harm. Employees would also be able to view or manipulate sensitive user data. It is better to use a one-way hashing algorithm to securely store passwords in a hash that can be verified using the same hashing algorithm.

However, there are many different one-way hashing algorithms available and some are significantly better than others. In his famous **blog post about password schemes**, Thomas Ptacek walks through the typical simple hashing systems that naive engineers implement and how terribly bad they are. He even links to a super cheap FPGA implementation that can break even the most complicated MD5, DES, SHA1, and SHA256 hashes in no time at all. Thomas calls it the "game-over" hack.

SOLUTION

BCrypt was designed specifically for hashing sensitive strings like passwords.

The **Node.js BCrypt implementation** has been around since 2010. It has gone through numerous security and code **reviews** over the years (including by our very own Van Nguyen). Node-bcrypt makes it very easy to hash your passwords in a comparatively secure method:

```
var bcrypt = require('bcrypt');

// goes through 2^rounds iterations to generate salt
// higher numbers require SIGNIFICANTLY more time to
calculate
var rounds = 12;

var salt = bcrypt.genSaltSync(rounds);
var hash = bcrypt.hashSync(user_input, salt);
// Store hash in your password DB.
```

XSS

Cross-site scripting (XSS) is one of the most common vulnerabilities where a web page with a text form input blindly accepts arbitrary inputs from users and displays this input unescaped on another page. Attackers can use this to inject malicious client-side JavaScript that gets executed by anyone viewing the page.

See the **OWASP XSS webpage** for a more detailed breakdown of the many ways an attacker can take advantage of XSS.

SOLUTION

Use leizongmin's popular **js-xss** module. The xss module will escape input strings and prevent most, if not all, of the common XSS vectors quickly and conveniently.

```
var Joi = require('joi');
var Xss = require('xss');

var config = {
    validate: {
        payload: {
            name: Joi.string().required().min(1)
        }
    },
    handler: function (request, reply) {

        var name = Xss(request.payload.name);
        return reply(name);
    }
};

var Joi = require('joi');
var Xss = require('xss');

var config = {
    validate: {
        payload: {
            name: Joi.string().required().min(1),
            email: Joi.string().optional()
        }
    },
    handler: function (request, reply) {

        var output = {};
        output.name = Xss(request.payload.name);
        output.email = '';
        if (request.payload.email) {
            output.email = Xss(request.payload.email);
        }
        return reply(output);
    }
};
```

Recall from Chapter 5 that **joi** can validate our inputs and output. As you can see in the above example, combining **joi** with **xss**, we can make our inputs secure to prevent against these types of attacks.

CSRF

Cross-site request forgery (CSRF "see surf") is another common vulnerability where an attacker is able to insert a script or link (using XSS) that causes the victim's browser to submit a form on a distinctly different but familiar website such as their bank website. If the victim has unexpired cookies to that bank website, the form may be blindly accepted as if the victim intended it.

SOLUTION

The bank website should generate a custom identifier on form load that is required in order to submit the form. Any blindly submitted form payloads will be rejected without this key. The victim would have to visit the form, fill out the elements, then submit in order to perform the attacker's desired effect.

Use hapi's **crumb** module.

```
// Server
var crumbOptions = {
    restful: false, // false enables payload level
validation of crumb, true uses X-CSRF-Token header
    addToViewContext: true, // automatically add to view
contexts
    isSecure: false // required if HTTPS is not used
};
server.register({ register: require('crumb'), options:
crumbOptions}, function (err) {

    if (err) {
        throw err;
    }
});


// View
<form action="/submit" method="POST">
    <input name="crumb" type="hidden" value="{{crumb}}"/>
    <!-- ... -->
</form>

// POST `/submit` Handler
handler: function (request, reply) {

    return reply('ok'); // Do not have to do anything
```

```
differently
}
```

SSL

Many websites today run on bare HTTP instead of the more secure HTTPS. This performs all of the data transfer between browser to server in plain text on the network. Due to the way networks work, anyone on same network can view all of the data transfer traffic and see passwords, URLs, messages, and more.

One of the easiest ways to add more security to a website is to force users to use SSL/HTTPS. This requires buying and installing certificates, but it will encrypt all of the traffic between browsers and servers.

There are many ways to configure SSL for a Node.js based web service. The most common way is to use a reverse proxy like Apache or nginx/stunnel to handle the SSL certificates, terminate the encryption, and then forward the traffic to your Node.js service over unencrypted HTTP. This requires no change to a working HTTP hapi application. For information on how to use nginx ssl termination, see **DigitalOcean: How To Set Up Nginx Load Balancing with SSL Termination**.

Alternatively, Node.js can terminate the encryption by processing the certificates, but this can be time consuming and increases the load on application machines. For information on how to use hapi SSL termination, see the **API docs** under server.connection's `tls` option. Below is a basic example of enabling SSL termination in hapi:

```
var Fs = require('fs');
var options = {
    port: 443,
    tls: {
        key: Fs.readFileSync(keyPath, 'utf8'),
        cert: Fs.readFileSync(certPath, 'utf8')
    }
}
server.connection(options);
```

Header stripping

There are may vulnerabilities that can be fixed by either setting or removing an HTTP header. Before breaking down the various vulnerabilities, here is a generic way to globally set or remove headers:

```
server.ext('onPreResponse', function (request, reply){

    if (!request.response.isBoom) {
        request.response.output.headers.toAdd = 'someValue';
        delete request.response.output.headers.toRemove;
    }

    return reply();
});
```

Alternatively, this can be done within a single handler to apply to just a single route:

```
handler: function (request, reply) {

    return reply(output)
        .header('Content-Type', 'application/json')
        .header('X-Frame', 'DENY')
}
```

CLICKJACKING

Clickjacking occurs when your web page is inserted into an HTML iframe where users' clicks can be hijacked. If a user clicks on your home button, an attacker could hijack the click and redirect the user to a malicious webpage.
Solution

Setting the X-Frame header to 'DENY' will prevent browsers from allowing your webpages from being put inside of a frame or iframe (<iframe>).

X-POWERED-BY

Most web server frameworks will, by default, announce in the HTTP header "X-Powered-By" what framework and version was used to generate the page.

By default, hapi does not do this. But, if you publicly blog about your hapi tech stack, your attackers will also see that.
Solution

A common way to mitigate the risk of being open about your tech stack is to provide a middle-man proxy in between you and your users. Popular choices are **CloudFlare**, **Fastly**, and **Akamai**.

IE OPEN WITHIN CONTEXT

Internet Explorer 8 fixed an old vulnerability where an attacker could open a remote or local HTML file within the security context of your site to run malicious code. To read more about the issue, please read the **Microsoft Blog Post**.

Solution

Setting the 'X-Download-Options' to 'noopen' will prevent this issue in Internet Explorer 8 and up.

contentSecurityPolicy

Technically, by default, browsers will allow you to embed arbitrary Java-Script (via script tags) from any domain. This is normally acceptable. However, it possible that a developer entering a typo into their code could cause the wrong file to load and execute malicious code.

Alternatively, if the web application allows for users to specify their own JavaScript to embed on the page, managing security can quickly get out of hand.

SOLUTION

Modern browsers now support a system called Content Security Policy. By returning a bunch of HTTP headers, it is possible to force the browser to create a whitelist of acceptable domains and restrict script-src calls to just this list.

Use **blankie** in combination with **scooter** to quickly define CSP rules.

```
var Hapi = require('hapi');
var Blankie = require('blankie');
var Scooter = require('scooter');

var server = new Hapi.Server();

server.pack.register([Scooter, {
    plugin: Blankie,
    options: {} // specify options here
}], function (err) {

    if (err) {
        throw err;
    }

    server.start(function(){
```

```
        console.log('server started');
    });
});
```

CORS

By default, a modern browser will prevent AJAX calls to any domain that does not match the current page's domain. This is because major web browsers enforce a **"Same-Origin" policy**. This Same-Origin policy is a critical aspect of web security.

However, as a developer, you might *want* to allow your web application to directly access a third-party API, or even your own API but on a different domain.

CORS, **Cross-Origin Resource Sharing**, allows you to do this in a safe and secure manner by explicitly specifying to which domains the browser is allowed to connect to via AJAX. This is done by sending custom headers to the browser on response.

SOLUTION

hapi supports CORS out of the box, but, it is disabled by default for security. Enabling it is as simple as setting the 'cors' server option to `true` or passing it a configuration object with one or more allowable 'origins'.

```
var serverOptions = {
    // ...
    cors: {
        origin: [
            'http://localhost:8080','
            http://localhost:8000'
        ]
    }
};
var server = new Hapi.Server();
server.connection(serverOptions);
```

In hapi, CORS can also be applied on a route-by-route basis:

```
server.route({
    method: 'GET',
    path: '/custom-cors',
    cors: {
        origin: [
            'http://localhost:9000',
```

```
            'http://localhost:8000'
        ]
    },
    handler: function (request, reply) {

        return reply("This response has custom CORS headers
set.");
    }
});
```

With CORS configured, hapi will set the correct headers automatically. Then, your client-side applications can safely and securely access your origin hosts.

crossdomain.xml

As mentioned above, CORS allows web application developers to control which domains their client-side JavaScript can make requests. Some applications use technologies that CORS does not filter like Adobe Flash. For Flash, Adobe has defined a cross-domain policy file, **crossdomain.xml**.

SOLUTION

```
<?xml version="1.0" encoding="UTF-8"?>
<cross-domain-policy xmlns:xsi="http://www.w3.org/2001/
XMLSchema-instance" xsi:noNamespaceSchemaLocation="http://
www.adobe.com/xml/schemas/PolicyFile.xsd">
   <allow-access-from domain="your_domain.com" />
   <allow-access-from domain="your_other_domain.com" />
   <site-control permitted-cross-domain-policies="master-
only"/>
   <allow-http-request-headers-from
domain="*.your_domain.com" headers="*" secure="true"/>
</cross-domain-policy>

var Fs = require('fs');

server.route({
    method: 'GET',
    path: '/crossdomain.xml',
    handler: function (request, reply) {

        return reply(Fs.readFileSync('./
crossdomain.xml').toString());
```

```
    }
});
```

Summary

In this chapter, you have now seen how to use hapi to defend against the most common web security vulnerabilities.

Review

In this book, we've gone through a quick introduction to hapi. We've learned how to set up a server and how the request lifecycle works so that we can extend that to meet our needs. We set up routes, handlers and learned how to organize our code into smaller components for reuse and readability. Validation was tied in to enforce not only our inputs but also our output. Plugins organized our code and we learned that utilizing these can create efficiencies and are more beneficial to more traditional middleware approaches. We've learned to leverage the authentication plugins to enhance your application. We've shown some common model use cases and how to use templating for your application to separate your presentation layer in the handlers. Finally, we've shown how to test, debug, and add security to your application in order to make it production ready.

If you find yourself still needing help, hapi has a great **community**. There are many options in order to get help and the best place to start is found at **hapijs.com/help**. We encourage you to participate in the mentor program that is mentioned in the help page to make the community even stronger. Please be respectful by utilizing the **Conference Code of Conduct** so we can continue to have a great community.

Once you have mastered some skills, we encourage you to become an active participant to mentor others, help with issues by **contributing**, or support in any way that you can to continue to strengthen the community.

There are additional resources at your disposal to increase your hapi skills. There is a node school self-guided lesson called **makemehapi**. There are also **tutorials** and other **resources**.

We hope by reading this book, we've helped you get started on your first hapi project. You can use hapi to make your dreams come true and build all sorts of interesting web applications.

Appendix 13

Models

History

Scalable applications typically follow an n-tiered architecture where the application service connects to an orthogonal database (meaning it is not tightly coupled with the application service and can be managed independently or even swapped out completely).

Today, there are many databases available for use. There are three main classifications for databases:

- Relational (RDBMS)
- NoSQL
- Other

Relational databases are the workhorse for databases. They've worked effectively for decades and have proven performance characteristics. However, they do have a learning curve and are not always suited for handling sequential data, denormalized data, or seriously high performance requirements.

NoSQL databases are relatively new. Typically, these have a very short learning curve and have high performance characteristics. However, due to trade offs, they do not have all of the features typically associated with Relational databases (like transactions, atomicity, data durability, etc.).

Other databases may include graph data structure databases or anything else that does not fit the two above classifications.

Overview of HTTP Clients

HISTORY

When the Internet was still completely Web 1.0, most websites and companies did not provide developer-friendly APIs. To grab data from a website required developers to scrape the website, process the HTML, and search & extract data (sometimes manually). Some companies started offering SOAP APIs, which (thankfully) died out.

Web 2.0 applications became the new normal around 2004, which supported APIs with XML and **JSON** responses. Java strongly coupled and adopted XML. But with the ubiquity of JavaScript being everywhere and amazing open source libraries with AJAX that came out like jQuery, Dojo, Prototype, JSON basically won. JavaScript & Node.js play great with JSON.

Most APIs today support primarily JSON. Our examples show code for interacting with JSON.

To fetch data from HTTP APIs, we have a few options. We will cover two of the most popular options: Wreck and Request.

WRECK

Wreck is one of the official hapi modules written by our very own **Wyatt Preul**, a co-author of this book.

It was created in response to the now infamous **4 byte memory leak**. One of the culprits was an underlying piece of code used by the popular Request module.

Additionally, Request was designed to accomplish a wide range of use cases. Wreck takes the minimalist approach and provides only the bare minimum feature set to ensure high performance and no memory leaks.

REQUEST

Request is the most well known HTTP request module for Node.js. It was originally created by **Mikeal Rogers**, a very well known figure in the Node.js community at large, but now the project has grown a life of its own. It gained a huge following due to its simple, intuitive interface (it is light-years better than the previous long-winded way of manually creating HTTP sockets).

Overview of database clients

hapi-plugins.com uses MongoDB through Mongoose driver so primary examples will reflect this choice.

However, for maximum benefit, this book will also showcase separate examples for three of the most popular databases used in Node.js projects: MongoDB, Cassandra, and Postgres.

MONGODB

MongoDB is an explosively popular database. It was one of the first databases to embrace the NoSQL movement as well as the open-source development model. It is available for free under the GNU Affero license.

Unlike MySQL or PostgreSQL, MongoDB is a document-oriented database. Instead of storing a Person's data like names, addresses, etc separately, in MongoDB, these fields can be stored together in a single document for that individual Person. This is intuitive to work with.

MongoDB supports a simple but powerful JavaScript-based syntax for queries and has a very short learning curve. This makes MongoDB a popular choice for rapidly starting projects, for hackathons, and for teams already comfortable with JavaScript.

There are two primary downsides to MongoDB. Scalability is not linear and requires setting up mildly complicated replication systems. Write performance can be a problem due to database-wide locking and the default setting can potentially lead to data loss when writes are not verified.

For practical purposes, at the time of writing, the choice of MongoDB ORM/driver to use is highly controversial.

On the one hand, Mongoose is popular and has a lot of helpful features, however, at the time of writing, the Mongoose GitHub repository has over 400 open issues reported and almost 2000 closed issues. With so many bugs, it may not always be the best choice.

The mongodb driver is simple and effective but provides very little high level functionality so more development work is required.

mongodb

The **mongodb driver**, also known as node-mongodb-native, is the most popular library for accessing MongoDB database instances. It fairly accurately mimics actual MongoDB syntax with some asynchronous modifications made as necessary. As such, it is less an ORM and more of a manual database driver. Therefore, intimate knowledge of MongoDB query syntax is required. Fortunately, MongoDB syntax is very simple and easy to get pick up.

Mongoose

Mongoose ODM is a high level object resource mapper for use with MongoDB. Created by LearnBoost (now part of Automattic), Mongoose provides abstractions away from pure MongoDB syntax in an attempt to make development using MongoDB faster and easier by adding support for queued operations, schemas, schema validators, defaults, methods, etc.

CASSANDRA

Cassandra is another popular, open-source NoSQL database. Instead of focusing on ease-of-use for developers, like MongoDB, Cassandra focuses on using mathematics and science to give developers scalability and high availability (can survive multiple machine failures) all while exhibiting extremely high performance. It also focuses on simple linear scalability which means scaling up is as simple as adding machines to the cluster (no mildly complicated replication systems, everything is automatic).

Cassandra is a column-oriented database. Every record in the database can have any number of columns that serve as fields. Individual records can have a different number of columns. A Person object could have name and address while another Person has name, address, and phone number. Every one of a Person's columns is retrieved when read. Column databases may not be as intuitive as document databases but they have a lot of unexpected practical benefits (like being good with storing and managing graph data structures).

The primary downside with Cassandra is it's relatively large learning curve. It is hard to get started with Cassandra. However, once things are configured correctly, Cassandra's features and benefits are hard to match.

Apollo

Apollo, by 3logic, is an up and coming Cassandra ORM. Even though development on Apollo started relatively recently (mid 2014), it is already completely functional and compatible with the latest breaking changes to Cassandra's CQL interface. Technically, the authors do point out in their README.md that Apollo is 'incomplete' and probably not production ready. However, Apollo is far better than the existing alternative ORMs out there.

cassandra-driver

Cassandra-driver is the official DataStax node.js to Cassandra driver. It supports all of the latest features and is actively maintained. However, it offers little to no high-level features so some development will be required to create effective models.

POSTGRES

PostgreSQL is a very popular, open-source RDBMS alternative to MySQL or Oracle SQL. It offers many of the features of commercial relational databases despite being free-to-use.

Unlike MongoDB or Cassandra, PostgreSQL follows the relational data model. This requires relatively significant set up time for configuring data schemas and indexes. However, this also means data validation is done for free on the database-side (instead of on the driver/client side for the above NoSQL databases).

The primary downside of using PostgreSQL is the learning curve. The relational data model system may be difficult to pick up quickly and has a lot of idiosyncrasies regarding indexing, grouping data, etc.

pg

Like the 'mongodb' driver, the **pg** module, also known as node-postgres, is more of a driver than a full-fledged ORM.

Sequelize

Sequelize is a full-fledged ORM that supports many different SQL based databases including MySQL, MariaDB, SQLite, MSSQL, and obviously PostgreSQL. It supports full schema definitions & synchronization/migrations, relationships, promises, transactions, pre-fetching, and many more features. It is also robust and well-tested in production.

Connection

MONGODB::MONGODB

```
var mongodbOptions = {
    'connection': 'mongodb://localhost:27017/hapiplugins',
    'options': {
        'uri_decode_auth': false,
        'db': null,
        'server': null,
        'replSet': null,
        'mongos': null
    }
};
```

```
var MongoClient = require('mongodb').MongoClient;

MongoClient.connect(
    mongodbOptions.connection,
    mongodbOptions.options,
    function (err, client){

});

var MongoClient = require('mongodb').MongoClient;

exports.register = function (plugin, mongodbOptions, next) {

    MongoClient.connect(
        mongodbOptions.connection,
        mongodbOptions.options,
        function (err, client){

            if (err) {
                throw err;
            }

            plugins.expose('mongodbClient', client);

            next();
    });
};
```

MONGODB::MONGOOSE

```
var mongooseOptions = {
    'connection': 'mongodb://localhost:27017/hapiplugins'
};

var Mongoose = require('mongoose');

Mongoose.connect(mongooseOptions.connection);
// No asynchronous call:
//      Mongoose queries are automatically
//      queued until the connection made

var Mongoose = require('mongoose');

exports.register = function (plugin, mongodbOptions, next) {

    Mongoose.connect(mongooseOptions.connection);

    // The following is technically unnecessary
```

```
    //    require('mongoose') will now point to this client
    //    when required from any file
    plugins.expose('mongoose', Mongoose);

    next();
};
```

CASSANDRA::APOLLO

```
var cassandraOptions = {
    'connection': {
        'hosts': [
            "127.0.0.1"
        ],
        'keyspace': 'hapiplugins',
        // 'username': '',
        // 'password': '',
    },
    'options': {
        'class': 'SimpleStrategy',
        'replication_factor': 1
    }
};


var Apollo = require('apollo');

var client = new Apollo(
    cassandraOptions.connection,
    cassandraOptions.options
);

client.connect(function (err){
    if (err) {
        throw err;
    }

    // client is now connected
});

var Apollo = require('apollo');

exports.register = function (plugin, cassandraOptions, next)
{

    var client = new Apollo(cassandraOptions.connection,
cassandraOptions.options);
```

```
client.connect(function (err){

    if (err) {
        throw err;
    }

    plugins.expose('cassandraClient', client);

    next();
});
};
```

POSTGRES::PG

```
var pgOptions = {
    'connection': 'postgres://username:password@localhost/
database',
    'options': {}
};

var Pg = require('pg');

var client = new Pg.Client(pgOptions.connection);
client.connect(function (err) {

    if (err) {
        throw err;
    }

    // client is now connected
});

var Pg = require('pg');

exports.register = function (plugin, pgOptions, next) {

    var client = new Pg.Client(pgOptions.connection);
    client.connect(function (err) {

        if (err) {
            throw err;
        }

        plugins.expose('pgClient', client);

        next();
    });
};
```

Postgres::Sequelize

Please note: Sequelize requires postgres related node modules to be installed:

```
$ npm install --save sequelize pg pg-hstore

var seqOptions = {
    'connection: 'postgres://username:password@localhost/
hapiplugins',
    'options': {
        dialect: 'postgres',
    }
};

var Sequelize = require('sequelize');

var client = new Sequelize(seqOptions.connection,
seqOptions.options);

var Sequelize = require('sequelize');

exports.register = function (plugin, seqOptions, next) {

    var client = new Sequelize(seqOptions.connection,
seqOptions.options);

    plugins.expose('sequelize', client);

    next();
};
```

Schemas

MongoDB::mongodb

Schemas are not really applicable when using the mongodb driver. For any applications that require some schema validation, please use Joi to provide some validation before inserting or updating documents.

```
var Joi = require('joi');

var internals = {};

internals.plugin = Joi.object().keys({
```

```
    'name': Joi.string().required(),
    'description': Joi.string().optional(),
    'version': Joi.string().required(),
    'authors': Joi.array().optional(),
    'license': Joi.string().optional(),
    'repository': Joi.string(),
    'homepage': Joi.string(),
    'updated_at': Joi.date(),
    'created_at': Joi.date(),
    'keywords': Joi.array(),
    'dependencies': Joi.array(),
    'dependents': Joi.array(),
    'stats': Joi.object().keys({
        'releases': Joi.string(),
        'downloads': Joi.string(),
        'downloads_this_month': Joi.string(),
        'open_issues': Joi.string(),
        'pull_requests': Joi.string()
    })
});


// Use it later
// var pluginToAdd = {name: 'hapi', ...};

Joi.validate(pluginToAdd, internals.plugin, function (err,
value) {

    if (err) {
        throw err; // invalid schema
    }

    var collection = mongodbClient.collection('plugin');
    collection.insert(pluginToAdd, function (err, result) {
        if (err) {
            throw err;
        }

        // success
    });
});
```

MongoDB::Mongoose

```
var internals = {};

internals.plugin = new Mongoose.Schema({
    'name': { type: String, required: true },
```

```
    'description': { type: String, required: false },
    'version': { type: String, required: true },
    'authors': { type: Array, required: false },
    'license': { type: String, required: false },
    'repository': { type: String },
    'homepage': { type: String },
    'updated_at': { type: Date, default: Date.now },
    'created_at': { type: Date, default: Date.now },
    'keywords': { type: Array },
    'dependencies': { type: Array },
    'dependents': { type: Array },
    'stats': {
        'releases': { type: String },
        'downloads': { type: String },
        'downloads_this_month': { type: String },
        'open_issues': { type: String },
        'pull_requests': { type: String }
    }
});

var plugin = Mongoose.model('plugin', internals.plugin);

var internals = {};

internals.user = new Mongoose.Schema({
    'username': { type: String, required: false },
    'name': { type: String, required: false },
    'email': { type: String, required: false },
    'updated_at': { type: Date, default: Date.now },
    'created_at': { type: Date, default: Date.now },
    'likes': [internals.plugin]
});

var user = Mongoose.model('user', internals.user);
```

Cassandra::Apollo

```
var pluginSchema = {
    fields: {
        'name': 'text',
        'description': 'text',
        'version': 'text',
        'authors': 'text',
        'license': 'text',
        'repository': 'text',
        'homepage': 'text',
        'updated_at': 'int',
        'created_at': 'int',
```

```
            'keywords': 'text',
            'dependencies': 'text',
            'dependents': 'text',
            'stats-releases': 'int',
            'stats-downloads': 'int'
            'stats-downloads-this-month': 'int',
            'stats-open-issues': 'int',
            'stats-pull-requests': 'int'
    }
};

var Plugin = client.add_model('plugin', pluginSchema);

var userSchema = {
    fields: {
        'username': 'text',
        'name': 'text',
        'email': 'text',
        'updated_at': 'int',
        'created_at': 'int',
        'likes': 'text'
    }
};

var User = client.add_model('user', userSchema);
```

Templating Engines

Overview of Selected Templating Engines

There are many templating engines out there. While the **hapi-plugins** application uses the most popular JavaScript-specific engine, Handle-bars.js, this book showcases examples for five of the most popular templating engines: Mustache, Handlebars, Jade, Dust, and ECT.

MUSTACHE.JS / HOGAN.JS

Mustache was created by Chris Wanstrath (of GitHub fame) as a "framework-agnostic way to render logic-free views". It strictly separates logic from presentation - it is impossible to include any logic in the templates themselves.

It is supported in practically every programming language. Thus, Mustache templates are highly portable and can be easily shared between projects of different programming languages.

As of 2014, the most popular Node.js Mustache compiler is **Mu**. But Hogan.js is gaining in popularity. **Hogan.js** is a blazingly fast JavaScript (supported by Node.js and JavaScript within browsers) compiler for Mustache templates.

HANDLEBARS.JS

Handlebars was created by **Yehuda Katz** (of Ruby on Rails, Ember.js, and jQuery fame) as an extension to Mustache. It is also actively maintained by **Kevin Decker** (of WalmartLabs).

Handlebars is designed to simplify writing templates by supporting expressions within tags (directly accessing subkeys of objects), partials (reusable fragments of a template), and helpers (JavaScript functions that can be used anywhere inside a template). These features make it easier to maintain large JavaScript applications with many templates. However, as such, Handlebars templates are not nearly as portable.

But, for hapi applications, Handlebars is, by far, the most popular templating engine.

JADE

Jade was created by **T.J. Holowaychuk** (of Express.js fame and was one of the most prolific Node.js module authors before retiring from Node.js). It was designed to be a "robust, elegant, feature rich" templating engine that borrows many concepts from Ruby on Rail's Haml engine.

Jade is designed specifically to template HTML content. However, unlike the other templating engines, it requires the use of custom syntax that differs from the output format (HTML). Thus, it has a bigger learning curve and effectively locks applications in to using Jade.

DUST

Dust was created by **Aleksander Williams**. It was designed to avoid the limitations of Mustache variants. It is asynchronous by default and composable. It has a similar syntax to Mustache and is highly customizable. Dust.js is used frequently by Netflix.

ECT

ECT was created by Vadim Baryshev. It claims to the be the "fastest Java-Script templating engine with embedded CoffeeScript syntax". ECT focuses on performance and quality-of-life development features such as automatic reload, JavaScript & CoffeeScript logic support in templates, multi-line expressions, and tag customization.